The Day the Gr
and other poems

Leo Aylen

The Day the Grass Came by Leo Aylen

Copyright © Leo Aylen 2012

First published in Great Britain April, 2012

ISBN for PRINT: 9780956892058
ISBN for EBOOK: 9780956892065

Cover image: © Leo Aylen
Printed and bound by: Shortrun Press

eBoook distribution by Faber & Faber

www.muswell-press.co.uk

for Pauline

Contents

The Day The Grass Came

The Norse god Odin is the speaker for most of the poem. In Norse mythology, the gods were mortal, and knew there would be an ending of the world when they were killed by, among other monstrous beings, the great wolf. Odin, the chief of the gods, went about on earth disguised as a human workman, and sacrificed one of his eyes in exchange for wisdom.

The day the grass came

1.

The day the grass came

I'd climbed to the top of the world
Asphalt gas tip volcano's crater of scum-covered tar
Sloping, slithering, down a solidified lake
To mini-gasometers squashed into rust
Squatting by scaffold bars wrenched into s's and squirms,
Railway lines jaggedly mounting black air
Tangled with cranes crooked over the dangling chains
Clanking on corrugated huts swaying high
On their tracery mounting, clunking on piles
And piles of ladders climbing themselves to confusion …
Everything leading to nowhere …

Railway sleepers lie scattered …

Rotten sleepers lie scattered,
Slumped in the rusty dust.

Sleepers, waiting for what?

Beauty sleepers, waiting for a Prince Charming kiss?

Sleepers, waiting for what?

For four angels to blow
Rolling the earth in a scroll?

No.
The trumpets and gods have gone.

Here at the top of the world
I sit alone
In my tar-stained overalls
Trying to focus my eye
Over the cities I advised
As I walked the world in my overalls
Learning how to be wise.

Through me the cities stand
Rectangular, perfectly planned
Tanks of concrete and perspex —
Live-tanks, learn-tanks, sex-tanks, play-tanks,
Beyond them the work-tanks, make-tanks, think-tanks,
And the tanks filled with monitor screens
For machines to watch over machines.
All tanks connected, computerized.
All tarmac, perspex, one-eyed, and wise.
All constructed by my advice.

Or was this really my plan
When I started to walk among men?

Here in this sacred place
Set aside for the worship of waste —
Olde-tyme rubbish-tip waste —
Not our ever-increasing well-planned waste-tanks
Filled to the top of their towers
With plastic cups, memo-forms, pay-slips,
Taking their proper place in a well-designed landscape —
But in this primeval place
That dates from the youth of the world
When men drove round in trains,
And I, with my heart full of steam engines,

Thundered to work every morning
In my dungarees and hob-nailed boots,
Shovelled the building sites,
Struggled to get my rise,
Sloshed concrete into the mixers,
Erected concrete silos, where once there'd been silos of grain,
Always building for men
Cities with giant-filled windows,
Where people could plunge like fish in clear water,
Like baths after work,
Play with the brilliance of plastic, the glitter of lurex,
Enter dream-worlds of three-dimensional,
Continually realigning, bright projections
In all the colours of rainbow and ultra-red,
With all the bleeps and whistles of sound
To add to their birdsong and fiddles,
With twenty centuries of the world's childhood
To play with, in many-faceted diamonds
Of view-palace, think-palace, play-palace, dance-palace,
City within city within city within city
Within projection of diamond-faceted dreams.
All this I planned in my jeans and Tuf boots,
Eating my bacon-'n-egg sandwich in the door of the chippies' hut.
All this I planned for the beautiful men beside me
Who sloshed the concrete over my Tuf boots,
And built suspension bridges over the estuary,
Teaching our roads to fly.

Or was this really my plan?

On the day the grass came
I sat by the sleepers of the sacred place
Consecrated to the unplanned, antique, waste,
And spat on the ways in which I learnt to be wise.

2.

Lord Manager sat on his swivel throne,
Surrounded by switches and thinkophones,
Bouncing emails by satellite
To make 'em arrive the previous night.
All the emails ever said
Was "Re your P. As B., take B as read."
His personal speech-module stood behind him.
To utter one word he needed a prompter.
"Repeat yourself" — it was there to remind him.
"Lord, Manager, always repeat yourself,
Or they'll kick you upstairs, leave you on a shelf."
But there's no upstairs.
Upstairs of Lord Manager's perspex think-tank
There's only the sky,
Where all fly-tanks and satellites
Are orbiting round Lord Manager's monitor eye.
For fifty-nine minutes every hour
Lord Manager demonstrates his power,
Broadcasts himself, surrounded by monitor screens,
His picture repeated a hundred times,
His voice-synth message: "Look, what man has achieved with machines:
IN-STANT COM-PUT-ER-IS-AT-ION."

On the day the grass came
Lord Manager sat at his swivel screen,
Digitised, synthesised, clean supreme.

3.

Then, just before the grass came,
I noticed one patch of green,
Right at the westernmost edge of the world —
Ultima Thule, last of the Hebrides,
Forgotten for thousands and thousands of years.
One green island had, after all, remained.
One man and his wife, alone.
Congenital idiots, deformed
By centuries' inbreeding,
Yet still alive, seeding themselves like grass,
Living in dry-stone croft.
No think-tank, work-tank, sex-tank, play-tank,
No tabletised eating.
They eat by chewing bagfuls of pounded grass-seed,
Baked with a mildew called yeast
Into brown crusty lumps called bread.
They shit straight into the earth,
Not the deodor bin.
They live as men did when the world was young.
This bent, deformed, ugly couple,
Squalid, and smelly, and old,
Spend their time crouched over their grass,
Building it dry-stone walls,
Shifting rocks with their own gnarled fingers,
Dunging it with a few sheep,
Throughout the winter, filling a vast leather book
With tiny pictures of all the different grasses —
Green Panick, Sweet Vernal, Cat's Tail, Marram,
Tufted Hair, False Oat, Meadow Soft,
Couch Grass, Darnel, Tufted Rye,
Barren Brome, Hairy Brome, Water Whorl,
Cock's Foot, Common Quaking, Squirrel Tail,
Silky Bent, and silvery Fog,
Barley, and wheat, and oats, and rye,
Pictured in thin, thin, colours by crippled hands,
Described with spidery writing in faded ink,

Pressed dry and buff on a dust-coloured page.
Grasses preserved in a book,
Grass kept alive on the Outmost Island,
Open as ancient dry-stone walls,
Grass like they reaped in the youth of the world.
Grass which idiots, bent by arthritis,
Have tended with ploughs of bone,
Bronze, iron, or steel,
Tended and watched till harvest.

I suddenly saw them, the idiots — bent, gnarled, by no means wise.
They have the use of both their eyes.

4.

Here at the heart of the world
Lie sleepers crumbling to dust
In a crater of scum-covered tar.

April gusts are frothing the air,
Frothing the steel-wire branches of cherry trees
To pink-an'-white blossom —
No. Cherry trees there are none.
Pink-an'-white blossom is none.
Steel wire tracery, split by the wind like leaves,
Brown fallen leaves of rust.
April's autumn breezes shift the flakes of brown iron.

April gusts are frothing the stream
Into kingfisher-turquoise and red-dappled trout —
No. Kingfisher, trout, there are none.
Effluent turquoised the stream,
Poisoned the air of the tiniest, red-dotted, fly.

But then, slow .. slow ..
On that gusty April day …
Slow .. slow ..
On that gusty April day …
Suddenly came the grass …
Slow .. slow .. slow .. and then faster …

First as green fishes swirling the asphalt lake,
Writhing, and swathing, and turning, and breathing the black
Air crawling with dragons of grass clawed up the ash-slopes,
Fly-catching lizards of grass flickering over the ladders,
Lightning-tongued grass licking spattering petals of rust,
And spitting out seeds of dragonfly humming-bird
Mayflies of grass spinning over the squashed gasometers,
Flinging the chains, and tossing the sleepers
Aside in a thunder of galloping bison, as rye,
Warm-blooded herds of rye,
Trample over the green springing plains.
Days squeeze themselves into matchboxes
To escape from this kangaroo grass.
Terrible seeds bombarding the perspex,
Where the last men cling to their speech-modules.
Time is crushed into wafers.
Grass seed vaster than vultures,
Pampas splits skyscraper ceilings,
Peels concrete off like paper.
Years flutter past like oatflakes.
Men flash out of wombs like skeletons centuries dead.

And the grass came,
Riding and mounting the earth
That man had asphalted —
Bullrushing grass, with loins inexhaustible,
Pumping its seed in endless ejaculation.

One by one the tiny museum mementoes
Saved from the childish world in their perspex cases
For occasional projection at Histry time on the screens —
Some columns called Parthnun, a spire called Chartker Theedle —
Writhed into clusters of tumulent growth,
While the rest of the tarmac and perspex
Smeared over the earth by me and the naked apes
Was kindly bulldozed by pampas and elephant grass.

Here at the heart of the world,
The black chrysalis cracked.
Gigantic butterfly green bright-falconed the air.
Polished the water clear.

There in the pale green stream
I saw my one-eyed reflection sneer
With a yellow-toothed wolf of a smile,
While I felt from my actual eye
Salt stinging tears.

5.

Instant Digitisation Lord Manager sat on his throne,
Surrounded by switches and thinkophones,
But all the rest of his empire gone.
He bounced emails by satellite
To make 'em arrive the previous night.
Now, marked urgent, the message said:
"Re your P. As B., take B as read."

Take B as red?
Take B as blue.
Take P as blue,
Take blue as red.
Take it as red, as blue, as black,
Take yer red message, yer black message back.

Takitas takitas takitas takitas
Tickyus tickyus tickyus tickyus ...

Grass burst out of the computer,
Burst through the hundred monitor screens.
Grass like the pounce of leopards,
Grass like the roar of lions,
Grass like the roll of breakers
Crashing the granite cliffs.

"Fetch my administrative assistant"
He screamed.
But with no speech-module word-pumping him,
His order came out
"Eh aye ah-initat ih-ah,
Eh aye ah-initat ih-ah,
Eh aye ah-initat ih-ah!"

No one was there to understand him.
Red Darnel pulsed through his swivel chair.
False Oat erupted out of his navel.
"Eh aye ah-initat ih-ah ..
Eh aye ah-initat ih-ah ..."

His cod-green slime eyes vaporised
To skeleton and marble slab.
"Eh .. aye .. ah-initat .. ih .. ah ...
Eh ... aye ... ah-in-it-at ... ih ... ah . . . . ."

Last slow echo from submerged speech-bank,
Disgorging discs like seeds ...

In rushed Chief Scientific Adviser,
Professor Purselips, famed for his study
Of the different intensities in children's urine
When fed on synthesised ice-cream or synthesised jam,
A work which won him the Nobel Prize,
Though the calculations were compiled by his assistant,
And all he actually did was piss by mistake in the jam.
But an email-writer second to none —
Except Lord Manager himself.
The room was dancing with Tufted Hair,
Squirrel Tail, Fescue, and Barren Brome.
Purselips was choking, but made an instant assessment,
Incisively issued his orders:
"Do something, someone" he screamed.
"Do something do something
Do something do something
Doosamy doosamy doosamy doosamy ... "

You, Purselips, you.

You do something. Watch.

Watch.
You, who are honoured with sacred title,
Most sacred title of all.
You, who are called . .
Scientist.
Knowledgist.
Wisdomist.
You
Have been called
To watch.
To die, watching Green Panick crumple a wall.
Contemplate Panick and die in peace.

Or at least
Measure the intensity of your own urine
As you panic to pieces …

But Purselips scrabbles his itching collar —
Wall Barley rears out of his hair —
Screaming in shriller and shriller and shriller soprano
"Doosamy doosamy doosamy doosamy … "

IN-STANT DIS-IN-TEG-RAT-ION.

Oats wave in the perspex penthouse.
Green Panick reigns supreme.

At last
Earth was avenged.

6.

Most of the naked apes died crouched in their home-tanks,
Glazed eyes glued to their view-tanks,
Or hunched in their drive-tanks,
Glazed eyes staring past work-tanks and think-tanks,
Dreaming of home and their own dream eat-tank,
Perhaps a cuddle in their own dream sex-tank,
Or strapped to their seats in a fly-tank,
Glazed eyes glued to a view-tank
Exactly the same as at home
And in all identical homes.
Out of the wash-bins, the cling-film eat-bags,
Burst, like Tyrannosaurus, the grass,
Like fanfares of parakeet, sea-horse, manatee,
Swallowtail, gibbon, and cobra,
Like Bird of Paradise snow white tail-feathers,
Like talons of plummeting eagle,
Burst like trumpets, like breakers, the grass.
Like antelope racing,
Like cheetah pursuing,
With all howls, whines, yelps, purrs, grunts, barks, snorts, roars,
Squeaks, whistles, and cheeps,
Contained in the marching rustle,
The race of the antelope-cheetah grass.
One moment a million million perspex containers.
One moment Lord Manager's Instant Civilisation.
Next moment the pampas
Steeple and skyscraper high.
Every pyramid
Truly grassed over.

Peace, peace at the end.
The earth avenged.

7.

There were still, dotted over the world,
Small beautiful men and women,
Who lay down at peace, for oats to breed in their bones.
Men who'd tried teasing ashes for a couple of seedlings.
Girls who'd reared tiny lichens from mould on synthesised cheese.
Some there were at whose death I was present:
Wild girl of Brittany, birdsong stroking your hair,
Blown down swift's wings in a swoop of twilight,
Blown down a kingfisher gleam to glow like reeds in a whirlpool.
You, my black friend, my neophyte impala,
Corn darting out of your eyes,
Happily washed into wind over ripening mealies.
And you, who once ran to catch at my breath and my hand,
Melt me the mirror, show me death's kingdom,
Tear out my eye …
And leave me gasping for blood in the lake of gold,
I saw you blown by the moon through the beards of the barley.

Peace, peace at the end.

Only the ultimate island
Lay as it always was:
Sheep-cropped grass and dry-stone walls.
Unchanged by unchanging time.
The man and his wife lay dying.

"Our love is a habit like bread.
We are twisted together with thorns.
Silence and space, and your eyes.
Grass will rise up through our bones.
Wherever we lie,
We lie in each other's arms.
Together we've grown.
Together we fall dead."

8.

My time was up.
Out of the thicket that had been Lord Manager's think-tank
Came wolf in his dark-grey suit.
Claws of press-button,
Eyes of laser.
Click went his brain — click click,
As discs flicked — click into place.

Eh aye ah-initat ih-ah
Laughing, he sneered at me,
Grinned with his long yellow teeth.
This is the end of men
After the end of you gods.
But not the end of the earth.
That is the joke of it all.

Not in the spreading dust,
Not in the nuclear ash,
But in gentle, rustling, grass,
Grass, the butler of man.
That is the joke of it all,
The Doom you never foresaw.
You and your naked apes
Poisoned the butterflies,
Oiled over the fish-jumping seas,
Scummed, gummed, down the forests.
All was rationalised.
IN-STANT DIG-IT-IS-AT-ION.
Here is the consummation
A rational god like you
Who knows how to learn by mistakes —
Oh, I quite forgot, you're through,
Finished, washed up like men …

Still, you do have time to savour the joke.
Voilà — the Rationalised World
Waits, like a cordon bleu chef, upon men.
Granted there's no more birds,
No butterflies, no honey bees.
But the useful fruits of the earth
Are ripening fast for harvest::
Barley and corn and rye,
Wheat and mealies and oats,
Bristle-leaved Bent for cattle,
Wavy Hair for sheep —
Though cattle and sheep there are none,
Loaves there are none to bake.
No washerwomen elbows to knead,
No ovens to sniff in the morning.
Still, barley, and wheat, and rye,
Oats, and mealies, and corn,
Seeding themselves across the world.

That is the joke of it all.
That my dear Odin's the ultimate joke.
Pity you have to disintegrate now.
It's a joke you need time to enjoy.
I alone have the time.
But I can, alas, no longer speak,
Once you, the last intelligence,
Disintelligentify.
What a pity, the joke of it all:
IN-STANT GRAM-IN-IF-IC-AT-ION.
Ih ah ah ih ih ih aye oh.
Yes Odin, buck up and die —
Aaaaye!
Ih ah   ah ih ih ih aye oh
Ih .. ah .. ah .. ih .. ih .. ih .. aye .. oh
Ih ... ah ... ah ... ih ... ih ... ih ... aye ... oh
Ih .... ah .... ah .... ih .... ih .... ih .... aaaaaye ... ooooh

Other Poems

Bloody Refugees ...

A man is crossing the sand.
The waste spits up at him
Like an angry snake. His hands
Jerk upwards. He's so thin.

His clothes are like the dust.
Why is he coming here?
What could he want with us —
We, who cringe in fear

From all our visitors,
Then, once they have passed by,
Attach plague-bites like burs
To their sleeves .. watch them die ...

Who is this, crossing our sand?
Who dares tread on our waste?
We, who plant nothing, are damned
If we'll let anyone taste

Our fruitlessness. We guard
Our despond-dirt with the one
Passion left in our turd-
strewn backyard souls. Our fun

Is choking all jokers to death.
Now the traveller's near.
There's a smile on his face like a breath
Of wind rustling his beard,

And here we allow no smiles.
Wait! Now he greets us, and passes.
Strike him quickly ... A pile
Of stones ... Crows ... Trampled grasses ...

Belfast Incident

Aching with lust. But for whom? I stare.
Me — withered woman, gawping at crowds,
Drooling at soldier crotches … The heat
Inflates me. I scratch at my dress, I tear
At buttons. My body is screaming so loud
"Take me, some man." I cuff and beat

Myself. I rip my skin, draw blood.
I lean against a lamp-post, spit,
Cackle to myself. A mad old crone.
Dress torn, bleeding from where there should
Be a nice bosom cleavage, but
Breasts have shrivelled. My figure's gone.

The crowd shudders. A gap appears.
Uniformed men. Weeping. Heads turn.
The crowd ripples in waves. Six men
Carry a stretcher, like bearing a bier.
But the corpse is only wounded. I squirm
Between elbows. People-walls bend.

The stretcher brushes my groin. His wound —
Centre of the chest, exactly where
I scratched myself as my fingernails
Thrust my self-rape on me. Cocooned
In dying, he butterflies in the air
For a last smile — at me — then fails,

Falls, eyes gone rigid, staring-stiff.
In that flicked moment of leaping death,
I felt us join — the blood of our breasts
Blood-brother melding. Like sex. A gift
Of himself. His final snatching at breath
Was a smile at me, an answer of 'yes'

To my 'take me.' His bleeding killed him.
Mine is a silly scratch. No more
Panting at boys. I'll still be the mad
Old hag on the corner. But now my limbs
Are quiet, satisfied. His war
Is over. Mine too. We are both dead.

Water Witchcraft

The people gathered at the witching pool.
Most of the crowd wore blood-spattered smocks;
They carried scythes. The apple carts
Were drawn by mules, who patiently pulled
The long trains of bright wagons. Clocks
Chimed midnight. Some girls tore their skirts

Into strips, and then, waving their scythe,
Danced slowly down to the mill-pond, plunged
Their scythe in, letting it sink down,
Down, to the bottom. "Will Witchy survive?"
The whispers rustled. Two soldiers lunged
For the witch, a plump blonde wearing a brown

Badly stitched dress with many large holes
Exposing shiny skin to moonlight.
Wavering torches. The witch-girl screamed
Like some vixen who's slaughtered fowls,
Calling from the hill to cubs or mate.
"Now sing your filthy blasphemous hymn"

One soldier bellowed. The girl began —
Inaudible words — her quavering voice
Scratched out meandering fiddle tunes
With frequent pauses. Waving his hand
To beat time, the other soldier boy
Started to harmonise in a croon.

The crowd yelled rage. They clumsily rushed
At girl and singing soldier, tore
The girl's rags off her, slapped her bum,
Shoulders, thighs, face, and hurriedly pushed
Her and the soldier into the roar
And suck of the mill-pool. Beating his drum,

The first soldier prodded the crowd
To shove her further into the dark.
"Will she survive the test of the scythes?"
The crowd's mutter growing louder,
The mood darkening like smoke-murk
Smearing shadow on the silver sky.

Where had the crooning soldier gone?
Bubbles and foam spread on the surface ...
The crowd, silenced, watches ... Nothing ...
Then, plop and a shout, just as the moon
Pops out of the cloud, the mocked, disgraced
Witch leaps, naked, from the deep, holding

A scythe — the test thrust down on her —
High in the shadowed, silver, air.
Then walks on the sheen of soothed water,
Flaunting her sex to the sheriff, bare
Legs writhing in mockery. She snatches
Pondweed handfuls. Smug matrons' hair
Falls as if tugged from their heads. She catches
Strands, and scatters them like feathers
Of slaughtered chicks in a vixen's lair.

Goddess of Many Names

Astarte-Inanna-Hathor-Mylitta-Ishtar-Aphrodite. Ever since the Willendorf Venus, 24000 years ago, artists have attempted to portray her. She belongs to every continent, but is at her most powerful in hot climates.

Not only through foaming waves, but up
Through gravid loam, which heaved, and swelled,
And burst, in a fountain of growth, she came —
Brown-skinned Aphrodite, like a top
Spinning with dance, like golden bells
Pealing from dark temples, like flame

Which, as it spurted upwards, changed
To blossom and fruit in all the colours
Of lightning, all the scents and tastes
Of scorched rainbows, ice-fire. She reined
In the earth waves on which her followers
Rode leopard-back, and, shouting, raced

Along her shores of opening. She,
Twirling tornadoes round her, seemed
Still as the eye of a hurricane.
All mortal men — instantly seized
By struck-to-stone mouth-gaping dream
Of being chosen. Her disdain

Shown for lip-moistening councillors
Merely inflates their warped desires.
She flattens them to paper cut-outs,
While whistling up her warriors
Whose festival lights impudent fires
No councillor would dare put out.

Rich fools drool over the flickering prize
Of a dance with her across the stars,
Spew cash, but then stagger-stumble, plunge
Her precipice into cesspit pigsties,
Where she stuffs their flabby gobs with dung.

Tiger Love Affair

begun at a chance meeting in front of Douanier Rousseau's picture of a tiger.

The painted tiger peers through tall green
Liana-stripes. The varnished jungle
Glows, as the glass frame sucks reflected
Spectator-faces into the scene.
The tiger jaws quiver. Dream-hunger
For an adventure, that unexpected

Rush of the hunter — the woman, the man,
Their eyes mirrored in tiger glass?
But tiger charges out of his frame …
They scramble on to his back, their hands,
Entwining, become the tropical grass
Through which stalks tiger — stripes of flame

With tearing claws. The man, the woman,
Pour jungle out of their surprised
Lips as the tiger bounds through their kiss.
Rockslide of a roar. The tiger summons
His mate, and, streaks of slashed sunrise,
The great cats crash together. Bushes,

Huge trees, the whole forest, ablaze
With tiger-patterned fire. Through sparks,
And smoke, and tossing torches, ride
The man, the woman, down tiger-ways
Of passion — flashing light and dark
Streamers of rampage, deep inside

Each other, till tiger-kittens purr,
And stir, and fall asleep again.
Tiger stalks back into his frame.
Picture calms down. He within her
Talks to her dreams … She answers. Then
Both notice their eyes are striped with flame.

Chosen to Bear Your Child

When you returned, your skin was flame.
Flames in your hair, and flames for eyes,
While, as you walked, small trails of fire
Swished from your footsteps. "I was maimed"
You said. "Now I am whole. Disguised
With flesh before. Now I can appear

"In my real body." So beautiful
You were, and yet I knew that if
I touched you — merely a fingertip —
I should combust to ashes. Appalled,
I gawped at you in awe. "A gift"
You said, stretched out your hands. Heat ripped

My clothes off me in seconds. I bulged —
Stark naked, saw my breasts were glowing.
I looked down. All my abdomen —
Radiant — my womb like a light bulb
Fluorescing my belly, my organs showing —
X-ray translucence — glory squeezed in

Each millimetre of fallopian tube.
My belly was swelling as I looked.
The x-ray light — very gently — dimmed.
"My flame, your flesh" you whispered. "You've
Only to breathe — the child will walk
Out of your body. Look after him.

"He is your son — and mine." Then mist
Seemed to grow through your stretched fingers
Like honeysuckle flowers. I drifted
On such a scent of joy. I kissed
Your vanishing ... So .. wait ... Womb stirs ...
What will this child be? Was I lifted

So far up out of time, that birth
Of our son has to mean death for me?
I hear your flame-voice calling inside
My own mind "Stay on Planet Earth.
Half-human, half-flame, our child will be
A helper ... " And now ... it's time ... I tried ...

Happy Endings — Best Beginnings

We thought we'd reached the garden, thought
We'd found a strange green space called home
Flowing with blossom rivers, where swans
Brought sunrise to us, and the ripe fruit
Asked us to dance galliards with them,
While future and past smiled, looking on.

We took each other's hand and walked
Astonished through the red and gold
Curtains of racing leaves, with time
Catching its breath. Harvest-rich stalks
Of ripening growth; no trace of mould
Or blight; nothing but juice and cream.

This was the garden of love, we thought.
Enter the wind, sweeping away
Blossom and river, harvest and dance.
Mould sneered at ripeness, swans forgot
Sunrise existed. And new day
Stripped every tree of every branch.

The garden of love, green space called home —
Was it a dream? We woke and felt
Love, riding a wind that caught us up
On eagle wings, to a kingdom
Balanced on storm-clouds. We were held
High in a dazzle of blue, on top

Of whirling pinnacles, while white
Waves raced and plunged in the joy tide's drift.
Tide and wind, joined in exultation,
Painted the universe with light,
And finally gave us ecstasy's gift —
Love, both garden, and endless ocean.

The Disappearance Bird

Lark? Or blackbird? Or nightingale?
The song was none of these. High, clear ...
Transparency of a sunrise sky?
Soaring of speed like wind through sails?
Dazzle of sun-specks tingling the ears?
No, a disappearing, which floated by

Far over our heads, and then was gone.
How many minutes? How many seconds,
Had the song lasted? No one could say.
Anyone see the bird? Not one
Description? Nobody even reckoned
They'd noticed it pass, or fly away.

Now it was gone. Hard to recall
Exactly how the song went ... Lark,
Blackbird or nightingale — how many
Of us can recollect in full
Their songs? And this — far too much work
For normal ears ... That bird's uncanny

Cadenza ... Grab that song in flight
And transcribe it? Are any human
Ears ever acrobat enough to capture
That fragile essence enough to write
Man-music to divert winged rapture
Down flutes blown by pedestrians?

How to transcribe dumbstruck delight?

Solitary Daffodil in Snow Valentine

To be offered the song
Of a daffodil all on its own in the snow
Under a sudden sun
Sprinkling the white expanse
With glitter and gold:
While the white silence lies still,
The sparkles run
Like syllables coming undone
Randomly spilled
Over this glistening land
Until they become
The words of this daffodil song
Dropped into our hands,
The promise, now to be fulfilled,
That we will, my love,
Walk on the wind, and swim in the lake of the sun.

Lark Song Valentine

Like that lark song
Leading us high and higher,
Soaring in spirals of music
Up, up, that spire,
That vanishing point,
To which we aspire to belong,
May our song — never losing
Touch with this choir of wings,
This throng of fiery
Melodies chasing the sky,
And forcing the frown of the clouds
Apart with a cry
Of triumph — may it reach the sun
As the lark's has always done.

So What Is "Love"? — Sonnet

So what is "Love", when love has disappeared?
Can memory become a presence — actual
As a tree planted on a grave? Revered
Legend only? Or can the past be a factual
Entity like a house, garden, or coast?
If what we had was "Love," then on whatever
Meaning that word has, our love is no ghost,
No faded phantom, for "Love lives for ever."
That love we danced through — even helped create,
Since love can be created by mere receiving —
Does that love live still, in some redeemed state,
Free of the sin, reproaches, lies, and grieving … ?
Oh love, your pain is worst. But I grieve too.

Perhaps what I've just said is even true.

The Knight of the Round Table's Wife

tells him what she thinks of quests for the Holy Grail.

"You come in, say you've seen the Holy Grail,
And you, and all the others, took a vow
To go out on a quest — where? Hill and dale,
Moor and fen — where? You don't know. Bet the cow
Is about to calf. Lizzie, your daughter, who
You say you love so much has told us Slade
Asked her to be his bride. Wed? Without you
Standing beside her? Never. Some old maid
Watching her lover marry his second
Choice — That for your dear Lizzie? Grails, quests, wars,
Words like honour ... Oh, I know you're not fond
Of shovelling dung day after day; the chores
We take for granted, you grudge doing ... Tell
The King you're needed here, at home, to build
Your loving wife a bigger cowshed ... Well
I suppose you must go. If you're not killed,
Come home safe, get drunk, make a lot of noise.
Women! We do love you, though you're such .. boys."

Marriage? Bach's Double Concerto

for two violins in D Minor

for Patrick & Wendy

Let loose this music of blessing's energy.
Old gods are present — a laughing Green Knight,
A leprechaun or two — in the company
Of Johann's angels fiddling with this light.

Here in a dazzle of squirrel-scurrying
Child-scamper through the beech-woods hand in hand,
Part the bushes as — hush — the queen and king
Appear to lead this silver-jerkined band.

Here, whether hands together, or hands apart,
This couple touches always. Argument?
Mere stretto in the fugue. Heart beats with heart
Into cadences white with ornament.

***

Then these cloisters, cool with remembered pain,
Where glimmers of memory, hovering in the air,
Fashion an interchange of soul, mind, brain,
Into such union, luminous with prayer,

That pain, by being cherished, can become —
As each past wonder's radiance reappears
Through suffering's damaged fog — a sum
Total of blessing compounded from tears.

***

Back to the energy which never fails,
A total dance of union at high speeds —
Prestissimo triplets racing up their scales,
In which first one and then the other leads:

Mutual interdependence. The dance spins far,
Far, far out into a whirling energy
Of cosmic rays and hurtling stars.
The dance goes on, into infinity.

Double Funeral

A couple, both film-makers, who died of cancer within days of each other.

Like blurring vision. Unnoticeably,
Almost as if they'd never been there,
Like movie special effects ending —
Two people walking slowly away
From camera, down a long, straight, bare,
Path between fields of ripening

Barley, then, while the camera lifts
And zooms out, they slowly dissolve,
While camera continues lifting
And zooming out. A few leaves drift
In front of the lens. Some structure revolves,
Then judders to a halt. A breeze buffeting

Windmill-sails in brief gusts. We're now
Watching in helicopter long-shot,
When we notice the two lovers
No longer there — disappeared ... how
Did they vanish?
            So now, without
Any words of goodbye, any murmurs

Of leaving, of sickness — let alone
Telling us they were dying ... gone:
A story's inconclusive end
Without the final signature tune.
We grieve, sure, but we also feel conned
Of proper grief. Here, take my hand

As you both used to do. I'm holding
It out to the empty air. If I
Could catch you now, I should be scolding
You for slipping out like that ... My eyes —
I can't see through for tears. Come back ...
Our whole scene is ... fading to black.

Letter to William

William Cookson, editor of **Agenda**, champion of the work of David Jones, died in January 2003. Like his mentor, Ezra Pound, he was passionate about the poetry of Dante.

William, your death signals an era ending: —
Gentlemen-editors who, their taste unquestioned,
Shepherded eager, though uncomprehending,

Readers with quiet, but insistent, suggestion
Through the selva oscura of modernism.
Behind your charm you were sheer steel, a bastion

Against today's illiterate barbarism.
You were our link with that past generation
Who, gathered round their Muse's ample bosom

In the Fitzrovia George, drank inspiration
From her milk, and, sometimes, droplets of liquor
More Bacchic — Muse who, with Nazi invasion

Threatening Britain, pressed her poetic trigger,
And fired Macneice's, Connolly's, and Dylan's,
Words at the Hun Hitler's jack-booted wreckers.

You are our Connolly. Like his, your villains
Were those who imposed slavery on language
Rather than populations. But his talents

Served a more literate age. Our undistinguished
Babble of poetasters — will they notice
Your passing? Will there be shivers of anguish

To shake dust from their magazines, whose bloated
Blandness squashes us with boredom? But no quarrels
Here, no niggles. Simply praise for the undoubted

Triumphs of your long, debt-dogged, editorial
Career — and you had very, very, many.
May I choose just one personal victor laurel

To bind round your forehead, my special penny-
worth of tribute: you were the first to publish
David Jones's *The Sleeping Lord*. If any

Work of today survives, that will, to establish
Your place among the elite perceptive critics
Who can tell obscure gems from obscure rubbish.

So, William, are you now strolling the city
With David, or, guided by Ezra, panting
In childlike anticipation — infinity

Notwithstanding — indeed now nearly frantic
With excitement, as you meet, face to face,
The master of the masters — himself, Dante,
Servant of Him in whose will is our peace?

from Dante's Commedia

1. *Inferno* VI, 7 – 36: Dante and Virgil encounter Cerberus.

In the third circle, it is always raining —
Where I am now — a cursed cold weight of water,
A law of saturation ever unchanging,

A dark, dirty, downpour; huge hailstones clatter;
Snowstorms and sleet; atmosphere so polluted
That the soil stinks of the disgusting spatter.

Cerberus — mad dog — distortedly brutish —
Three pairs of jaws howling like hound-packs rabid-
ly over the people submerged, water-bloated.

Six bloodshot eyes, black jowl-beards grease-bedabbled,
Barrel of a belly, paws on which gigantic
Claws clutch the ghosts, flench their flesh-weave unravelled.

Yelping like curs, driven by the drizzle frantic,
Trying to shield one flank by exposing the other,
The sinners writhe and roll in sodden antics.

When Cerberus, that dragon of hell's gutter,
Spotted us, his jaws gaped, fangs bared, his muscles —
Each one of them — in constant quiver and judder.

My guide stretched out his fingers, grabbed big fistfuls
Of mud out of the bog, and quickly stuffed them
Down the beast's three vast gobs till they were feast-full.

A dog, wanting his dinner, ruffs and wuffs, then,
While gobbling it, grows quieter, stops yapping.
It's feeding-time which makes him act the tough one.

So — the foul mouths of Cerberus, whose snapping
And yowling may make these folk prefer deafness
To his thunder-demon growls, just for once stopping —

We pass on through the rainstorm-flattened, breathless,
Shadows, our feet unable to avoid treading
On their human-being-bodied substancelessness.

2. *Paradiso* XXXIII, 1 — 21: St Bernard's Prayer to the Blessed Virgin.

"Thou humble highest summit of creation,
Both virgin mother, and thine own Son's daughter,
In whom the eternal plan reached culmination.

Thou art she whom humanity's Creator
Made to be His maker, and was delighted,
Since thou hast so ennobled human nature.

Within thy womb the love was reignited
Through whose warmth, in the peace of the eternal,
This mystic rose of saints is germinated.

Here in heav'n thou art to us high noon's burning
Flame of love; down there, to those still with bodies,
Thou art hope's fountain in our life-time's morning.

Lady, thou art so powerfully ready,
Praying for grace without thy interceding
Is flying without wings, and will fail badly.

Thy generosity races to needy
Petitioners, and often works so smoothly
It grants their prayer before they've made their pleading.

In thee is mercy, piety, and duty,
In thy vast magnanimity's united
All that's good in creation, and all beauty."

Two Dreams after Reading the *Commedia*

1. The Self-prison

> Fitti nel limo dicon: "Tristi fummo
> nell' aer dolce che dal sol s'allegra,
> portando dentro accidioso fummo;
>
> or ci attristiam nella belletta negra."
> > **Dante,** *Inferno* vii 121 — 24

> Fixed in the slime, they say : 'Sullen were we in the sweet air,
> that is gladdened by the Sun, carrying lazy smoke within our hearts;
> Now lie we sullen here in the black mire.'
> > *Temple Classic prose translation*

The dungeon-stone sweats damp. We crouch.
The ceiling frowns, leans on our shoulders.
My mind pulls my gaze down to the floor.
Our rage has shrivelled to constant grouch,
Curse-mutter, frown. We appear older —
More bent, more warped, more aches, more sores ...

We curse our captors. How long? The weeks
Trudge past. Each day's a sack of lead.
Slowly the room shrinks. Our foul air
Shoves us down. Crawl! Sprawl! Stench: the reek
Of urine stains our dreams. My head
Is squeezed small by the stink. I stare

At cracks in the wall. One of us yells,
Screams, screeches, tears his hair, his face.
Is it me? Am I this mind-smashed howl?
Soul-burst, I can no longer tell.
I am this — which is not pure space,
This block, this not-air thing, this foul

Bundle of smells. We creep about,
Nose to the ground. Whoever screamed —
The screams have slumped to silence now.
Groan-mumble is all. My nose — my snout —
Stubs on the wall, the door. It seemed
The door was open. Yes. I cower

Back into the cell. But yes. The door
Has been open for a long time.
We locked ourselves in with our rage.
Slowly, stand up. Yes, I am sure.
We can walk out. I finger wall-slime.
Astonished, I step off the edge

Of safe despair into the dangers
Of living, with others, and me, the stranger.

2. Eighth Circle

Quivi venimmo, e quindi giù nel fosso
vidi gente attuffata in uno sterco
che dagli uman privati parea mosso.

Dante *Inferno xviii* 112 — 114

We got upon it; and then in the ditch beneath, I saw a people dipped in
excrement, that seemed it had flowed from human privies.

Temple Classic prose translation

Blinded and gasping, I'm stumbling down
Rough rocks of a broken barricade,
And finding .. beneath .. a crumpled mass
Of bodies floundering in brown
Sticky dung-stench. I cringe, afraid
To breathe in this sulphurous gas.

Who are these wallowing persons? I
Call out "Does anyone here know me?"
Cackles of maniac-misshaped
Laughter. "Oh we all do" one tries
To mouth, through sewage gurgles. "We
Wonder why you, ducks, have escaped"

Splutters another. Breathing is hard.
I feel myself choking. Somehow
I have to cross … How? Do I wade
This muck? More voices. Then — these words —
Sharp like an order: "Plunge! Down! Now!
In the filth!" Words to be obeyed …

I am swimming, struggling through weed,
Pushing the strands of excrement
Away from my mouth. Head out. Breathe
Foul gas, dive down again. My speed
Increases. To my astonishment
I do emerge, matted and wreathed

With streamers of sewage ... But the air
Is purer. Cliffs. Clean rock. I climb,
Scramble up, higher, higher. Sky.
Blue sky with little clouds, and there
Are birds again. Bedraggled, I'm
Nauseous. I vomit at my

Own stench. Where can I find a river?
I climb on up. Who were those people
Bogged in that sewer? Look! A stream
On the cliff-lip. Am I forgiven?
I strip naked and wash. I dribble
Clear water, and ... wake from the dream.

Wild Weather Mouth

Wild weather mouth, open your hills
Of eagle storm. Teach me your tune,
And when I've learnt your secret wells,
Balance the river on my bone.

Wild weather mouth, my source ran dry,
Until the sand twisted your name
Out of the skeletons under the sea
Who'd walked the waves of lava steam.

Wild weather mouth, I enter you
On owl's wings which are not afraid,
For, when your storm is still, the glow
Of your volcano will greet the bride,

And I am you, wild weather mouth,
Riding the river beyond the sea,
While you are me, the windblown moth,
The fallen leaf of the last day.

Running the Hill

Hill topped. One breath, one quick look round:
The solid earth danced and rejoiced,
Glad in the knowledge wings had been found
For him by the air, as he, poised .. poised ..

On the edge of a cloud, stepped off his hill
And gave himself to the bounce of the wind
Which scattered him thistledownwards till
The rush and hush of the river within

Him met the river which rose to meet
His wind-wings diving the flower-crammed sky.
He floated through meadows rippling with freed
Leaf-life spread which, as he raced by,

Laughed at his sudden-blest two-legged gait,
While he, blown down by the gift which the air
Gave to his hilltop head, cascaded
Himself on the plain of .. every anywhere.

Glimpsing a Golden Oriole

just as a ray of sunlight breaks through the trees.

This burning point, this diamond air,
This daylight star, this flowering ray
Of a microscopic sun. Here, where
This nanosecond swallows the day,

And time spins round a whipping-top
Which seems to rest on eternity.
Dimensionless point, but no stop —
Perpetual motion, velocity

Beyond all comprehension. Here
Something has poised me, like a toy
For a child to play with. I'm so near
The edge of everything, but joy

Itself is helping me to balance
On a twirling needle of tumbling now
Like bird-bee-thoughtless scattered pollens
On randy stigmas. We are how —

In one small aspect — cosmic light
Fragments itself into corporeal
Fingers, nose, ears, teeth which can bite
Apples. Us and that golden oriole

Glimpsed through those leaves, lit by that ray
Of dazzle … We are us, but we
Are also .. light made flesh. Today,
This moment, as light meant us to be.

An Archaeologist's Intuition

When asked what he did, Auden never said he was a poet; he used to say he was an
archaeologist, as that shut the questioners up.

"We're trying to catch the gasp of the ghosts,
And give it back to them, so that
They, for a dazzling moment, breathe
Enough to whisper one almost
Incomprehensible, but yet
Utterly clear, story, and leave

"Us with a memory like the dream
Of a chance which won't occur again.
Oh this does happen sometimes to us,
When we're invited to join their game,
Though they will not let us know when
Their scent will rise out of the moss,

"And the oak stump seem for a moment to smile,
Even, open a mouth to speak.
It's then we need to be poised to run,
For all ghosts move like a slippery eel
Swimming aslant in a spear-thrown streak
Under the darkness and so soon gone,

"With the rest of the story left untold.
The gasp, once caught, quickly dissolves,
Makes memory seem a deceitful trick ...
The moss congeals on the mud. The old
Stump-fungus crumbles, and we ourselves
Clutch on to a tangle we can't unpick."

Dark Energy: Sparrow and Spark

Everything in the cosmos develops from hydrogen. The universe's supply of hydrogen, though enormous, is limited. The galaxies of our universe are being driven apart by a force which astronomers call Dark Energy. When the hydrogen eventually runs out, stars, galaxies, everything, will become cold and dark.

King Edwin of Northumbria invited some Christian missionaries in to his hall. Coifi, the pagan priest, noticed a sparrow flying through the firelight and out into darkness, and compared human life to the flight of the sparrow.
As recorded in Bede's *Ecclesiastical History*.

The sparrow flew out of the frozen dark
Over thegns thronging their mede-hall
To warm their guts with mutton and fire.
And then the sparrow was gone, like sparks
Which, popped from flaming timbers, fall,
Grey ash-specks on the black trampled floor.

Coifi, the pagan priest, likened
That sparrow's flight to the life of a man
Thrust from darkness up into a brief
Flutter through lighted warmth .. and then
Forced back down into the darkness whose hand
Is ashes to annihilate loss .. grief …

We who've sent humans to walk the moon,
Who chatter across the stratosphere
About the price of sun-cream, try
Hard to forget we're only clones
Of that small shivering sparrow … We're here
To spark like sparrows, then blacken, then die.

The Katowice Snowflake

On the night of Saturday, January 28th, 2006, in a conference centre in Katowice, southern Poland, where a crowd had collected for a festival of homing pigeons, the roof collapsed without warning, killing over sixty people. There had been a heavy snow-fall, and, although the building was only seven years old, the weight of the snow, which had hardened to ice, was too much for the structure. The midnight temperature of minus 15 degrees Celsius caused many of the trapped and injured people to die of cold.

Diamond flowers — once water, now jewels,
Feather-light floating down from grey sky
On to a micro-second dazzle
Of knifing moonlight. Voilà. Look! Cruel
Mass-murderers, hammering steel through eyes
And brains, transforming happy bustle

Of gossiping crowds into iced corpses —
Severed hands, arms, legs, congealed blood —
Crushed under concrete and midnight frost.
Without warning, the roof collapses.
Steel beams snap like dry thorns, and cut
Laughing crowds into shreds. The glass

Shatters — to jewels? Ice dagger spikes
Stabbing with impartial precision.
Children, parents, grandparents, scream.
Pigeon-winged blood gushes through shrieks
And clotted feathers. Iceberg collision's
The end of this sweet snowflake game,

While snowflake demons, viciously pretty,
Smear ice-age over the wounded city.

Pompeii

Cloud like a vulture — sooty black;
The cloud, swooping — black sliced with gold —
A bird with wings wide as a storm:
Lightning exploded out of its beak.
It dived, the scuttling people called
Out at deaf gods. The prosperous farms

Crumpled to clinker. The human ants
Jittered and skittered down flaming roads,
Where eagle wings were kindling the trees,
And vulture claws were ripping the tents
Where traders had sat, attracting fat crowds,
Whose faces, as though from sudden disease,

Flaked into ashes. The storm-bird's claws
Tore, scored, through houses, temples. The walls
Were blood spurtings, and jagged wounds
With suppurating gangrene. Cows
Solidified to statues. Howls
Of pain were sculpted in instant stone.

Vulture clouds hover over the still
Sudden silence of drifting smoke.
The deaf gods stroll up black ash hill,
Chuckling over their latest joke.

Volcano Aftermath

Clouted by cloud. The darkness weighs
Down on us like a dust-clogged heap
Of mouldy blankets. How can we breathe
These claggy fumes? Once the sun's rays
Flowed, beaming energy. Now we scrape
Stale soil from the stale air with our teeth

Like scaly creeping creatures. We
Have shrunk under this cloud to crawling
Insects, our skin a crimped beetle shell.
Will the sun ever return to free
Us from this weight of smoke lumps, fouling
Our bodies, our minds? Which vision of hell

Is truer? This dull blanketing
Of all we are or have with dirt
And gritty darkness? Or the flames
Which leapt up through the earth's thin skin
Pretending to be the sunlight's heart
Bleeding in scarlet lava streams?

Saved from a burning death? Some joke.
We have been saved .. to choke on smoke.

Haida Burial-pole

In the Queen Charlotte Islands, all that remains of a village destroyed
by smallpox.

The distant bay curves out into space.
The shore is littered with giant trees
Storm-stripped to silver matchstick — cedar,
Hemlock, and spruce. Humans, displaced
By this vastness, have heads like peas,
Limbs like grass-stalks, in this unweeded

Garden of a forest, which wraps the bay
In its dark hunting silences ...
Our eyes blur, searching rock, stone, sand,
At an ocean edge which oozes its way
Over the forest debris. Softness
Of moss tugs us like a child's hand

Back up and into the pillared hall,
The great cathedral, of these cedars.
Nothing remains of the village,
Except for one split burial-pole,
Pisa-tower-leaning, dragged off course
By tugging fingers of greedy sedge

And creeper that struggle up any ladder
Offered to reach the distant light.
One cracked tree-trunk, each year losing
A little more of its human odour,
Until the plants and beetles have quite
Obliterated everything

Which bears the trace of human craft.
Here were no Pharaoh-pyramids.
The people who built this settlement
Knew very well how utterly daft
It is for men with pea-sized heads
To think their work was ever meant

To last much longer than a moth's
Life. They carved poles from volatile wood,
Then watched grasses, fungi, and moss,
Smudge their carving ... and thought that good.

Fire: 200,000 B.C

1. Mother & Baby

Crouched in a hollow of heather hill,
I sit hunched like a mother ape
Nursing her baby. But this is more.
This is the life and death thing. Will
You live? Don't die … You're changing shape
All the time. Can you breathe? You snore

Sometimes, roar sometimes. You can grab
One end of a branch, and sharpen mere stick
To killing spear. You can wrap flesh
Of stag or duck, lobster or crab,
In greasy crusts that offer licks
Of gluttonous dribble. You can crisp fish

From watery stringiness to meat.
But you yourself are hungrier
Than any beast. Whole trees you'll gobble
Sometimes. Sometimes whole forests … Eat
These twigs, red mouth. I'm squatting here
To feed you morsels, tasty nibbles

Of wood and peat, to keep you alive
Until our weary hunters return.
Rest, little red serpent. Soon we'll feed
You fat branches; they'll make you thrive,
And make the stag's flesh dark and firm,
So you and I both glut our greed.

2.: The Stumbling Stranger

Our fire — dead! Cold ash … Stranger arrives,
Stumbling through bracken, his legs torn, ripped,
Bleeding, chest hammered, lungs rattling —
"Why so frightened?" He mumbles "Knives"
Drops at our feet. How his hands gripped
That bundle of turf with the thin, smoking,

Wisp of hope .. life … Now, once again
We needn't tear at the stag's raw flesh,
Needn't shiver in the drizzling night.
"Will 'Wounded Runner', our instant friend,
Surprise saviour" — the voices hushed —
"Will he survive, or will he die?"

Oh yes, we'll thank him, if he recovers …
While he lies helpless, we'll catch the broth
Dripping from our roasted venison,
Dribble it through him … Will — wonder — he weather
The blood-storm flooding him, clutching his breath,
And drowning him in his own ocean?

But if he dies — well then, we'll feast
On roast deer meat, sparing one brief
Moment of questioning who he was,
Who had attacked him. While some priests
Chant for his corpse, we shall grin, sniff
The cooking scent, jeer at the frost.

3. Me the Thief

Scratched and bleeding, spattered with mud,
I stagger into their circle — Fire.
They're huddled in furs, but they are warm.
I'm shivering — scanty rags, dried blood
On legs and arms, cuts on my ear,
My ribs, my back. My body's torn

And strain-wrenched. I crave sleep. To curl
Up in a fur, near those red embers.
I gobble the scent of roasting stag.
These people, whose language sounds like yells
Of pain, have welcomed me — The Stranger ..
Hot meat smells. Children touch my legs,

Stroke my hair, like fondling their dog.
The fire heat's calming my body's judder
And tremble. They pour some rich brown broth
Into my mouth — it's like the shock
Of blows to the head, this kindness, this utter
Lack of suspicion ... I was near death.

Now I can eat and sleep, begin
To think as human, not panicked deer
Kicking at knives and snapping hounds ...
But not for long. Before a hint
Of daylight peeps between the stars,
I have to steal their fire, crouch down,

Crawl through bushes and reeds, clutching
The precious embers wrapped in turf,
Until I reach the forest, then run.
And once again tear brambles, fling
Myself down gullies, dodge gorse and furze,
And — no pause at the river — lunge

At the sucking ford and stumbling rocks,
Holding the precious jewel of life,
The clutched turf with red breathing heart,
High over my head. Will my thief luck
Cheat the pursuit, and land me safe
Back in my children's familiar dirt?

Will I, once more home, tell my tale
And calm their shivers? Or, this time, fail?

Incident at Llanafan-fawr, Powys, in 1842

"Pine trees rustling. Needle-strewn path.
Darkness, with slashes of silver shimmer.
A glade. Full moon. I feel the hair
Stand on my arms, my chest. Black wrath
Muddies my sight. Lead heartbeats hammer
My ribs. My ears lunge at the air.

"A drowsy numbness? This is no Keats
Nightingale time. I try to quote.
'No more roving by light of moon'
Comes out as a cough, a growl. My feet
Burst through my shoes .. Hairy .. My coat
Splits. Arms grow leg-long. Scents balloon

"Around me. I see with my nose.
Roots and bark pass me messages.
I sniff moss. Wordlessly I learn
Huge secrets. The old black anger grows
Vaster inside me. Run. Howl. Yes,
Running .. but where? The darkness burns

"My belly. Howl. Run. Sniff the wind's
Silence. Somewhere I'll find … but what?
Square shapes .. strange smell .. a memory
Of softness … Leap. Square hole, strengthened
With bars. More smells. The female, hot
Writhings .. what sweet yelps .. easily

"Mounted .. and yet, a further need.
My teeth. Her neck. I drink the blood,
Float into her, swathed in rich dreams
Of womb-warm love, and growling seed.
Then blackness crashes down, and shuts
My nose-eyes, mind-eyes … sleep of screams … "

Next morning Bryn, his face streaked, splattered
With blood, was wandering round the farm,
Howling like hounds. His wife lay dead —
Carotid artery slashed, neck — tattered
Skin rags. Neighbours raised the alarm.
Bryn, tried for murder, howls, never said

Another word for thirty years
Of madhouse life imprisonment.
Well … murder weapon was never found.
Why marks like wolf fangs under her ears
And chin? And what were those footprints
Of a huge dog on the damp patch of ground?

The Bodmin Beast

Mist on the moor. Our feet squelch, squelch,
In the sucking bog. Wind. A fine spray
Spits into our blinking eyes. Hands grope —
Stumble — for granite outcrops, which bulge
Like monster heads out of the grey
Wet bent, the soggy peat's brown soup.

Mist on the moor. Now the dogs howl.
We reach the summit. Ravens bark.
Then — like film music, a screeching chord —
Farmer's wife shrieks "That was my foal!"
Sprawled legs, head, like .. a rug? Those marks —
Claw-slashes, four inches long — scored

Through neck, flank, belly — or, rather, through where
Belly, flank, neck, used to be ... This
Is no mauled carcase left by fox,
Badger, or dog. Mere skin, stripped bare
Of every shred of flesh. No mess.
Clean butchery. Recovered from shock,

Farmer's wife says "This was the beast
Of the moor. It has been known to lift
A calf over a hedge." We walk
Wearily down to the pub ... A fleece —
What's left of a sheep ... We drowsily sift
Through farmers' reports. All the moor talk

Is of the beast: Puma? Panther?
Leopard? Some huge wild cat, exotic
Killer ... Night-time ... The moor outside
Looms like nightmare ... Next morning we learn
A man from the ministry's coming. Emphatic
Assurance — all evidence will be weighed.

But — no, this man from the ministry won't
Walk on the moor, examine farmers'
Calf corpses, defleshed like burst balloons.
He'll just read documents. "We don't
Need chalk-stripe-suited varsity charmers"
Says Farmer Mike, who now reckons

He's lost sheep and calves worth a grand,
"We need a gypsy tracker, who smells
Peat-bog. These men from the ministry
Wear aftershave, they're too clever, and
They'll say 'Unproven' .. But you tell
Me — are those slashes imaginary?"

While other ministries implement
Insane decisions to bulldoze hills,
Then cover England with traffic cones
And orchid-obliterating cement,
The beast stalks Bodmin moor, and kills.
Puma? Panther? Leopard? Figment

Of Cornish imagination? ... We all,
Who, with our cars, our fellings of trees.
Our sprayings of garden insecticide,
Have done our bit to shave earth bald,
Need your claws, Bodmin beast, to seize
Back some small wilderness. So, hide

In the mist, beast, and at midnight
Rip the darkness with your yow-owl,
And, real or not, stalk our nightmares,
When the Earth, we humans have almost — not quite —
Like killer-pumas disembowelled,
Gives back to the beasts what once was theirs.

African Mask

A shabby Nigerian town's neglected museum; the only notable object a priest-goddess mask.

The mask hangs on the scabbed, cracked, wall,
A tangle of hair and beads. The eyes —
Holes, wells, fountains, of darkness — gush
Rivers of sooty silence, which call
Me to duck into their barely disguised
Realm of power. I stand there, crushed

By such silence, such darkness ... Now
The mask appears to move, to sway,
Pendulum-like. The wall's hair-cracks
Open to mountain chimneys. I bow.
Did the mask nod .. slightly? The play
Of sunlight over odd artefacts,

Like beads, bells, British coins, wine-glasses,
And two brass taps, swirls into one
Shimmering dangle of ornament
Sucked down those eye-caves where man passes
At his peril. Gods can have fun
With the shaking knees and excrement

Of a panicked human ... Wait. The mask
Hangs like a giant's anger. Revenge
On those safari-suited chaps
With polished boots, elephant tusks
Carried before them? Should I cringe
And crouch apology? I clap

My hands. Echoes … I sway my hips
As if beginning to dance. I stamp
My feet and clap again. A beat:
Stamp, stamp, and clap, clap, like dance steps
Dropped from her eyes' black pits, her lumps
Of coal darkness, threaded with beads

Of sunlight glitter, whose alive void
Jerks my feet-stampings like puppet-strings.
I dangle from Mask's invisible hands.
Her anger for her ritual, destroyed
By the pale-skinned jolly-good chaps, can sting
Like hornets, strike like cobras, and slams

My mind down through the floor with hammer
Blows — I become a wooden peg,
A nail, in the earth's coffin …Whose coffin?
My own. And now, as I sink — drummer,
Drumstick, and drum — my pounding legs
Faster and faster, Mask starts laughing —

Laughing, guffawing, rocking, huge bellows,
Spluttering chuckles, torrents of tears
Like sudden mountain-stripping flash flood …
Till Mask, sated, wades through the shallows
Of her great river, thrusts a spear
Into my belly, and guzzles my blood.

I flow down my own wound, escape
Over the lip of the waterfall,
And splash — crash — down into Mask's eye-pools,
Vanishing ... Some hours later, I scrape
Myself up from the floor, and crawl
Out, to find Time explaining the rules

Of civilised society:
Commuter trains and Internet.
Concentrate! Listen!
                    But did I see —
While trying to wipe away my sweat —
One of Mask's eye-holes wink at me?

Bird-woman Bead-woman

… but was I asleep? I seemed to be walking
Under a tangle of swinging branches —
They feathered my head; I raised my arms:
Birds flew up out of my fingers: squawking
Pied ravens, hornbills, twittering finches,
Bee-eaters. Bright feathers, bee-like swarms,

Changing, changing .. to strings of beads,
Scarlet. golden, colours of harvest,
As jungle shrank to a room. Surrounded
By orange and yellow, ochre and red,
I groped, sun-blinded … The tallest, furthest,
Tree bent, changed into a woman, who handed

Me her red heart on a dish of lips,
While beads and birds blurred into a halo …
I floated up flame flowers with her
Out through a sunset of jewelled sleep
Which sang like a golden oriole, swallowed
Both of us, till my clamouring thirst

Was quenched in the lake where she disappeared,
Leaving a bundle of beads on the shore.
I rose, and, still asleep, I peered
Over dawn's rim, afraid no more.

Ocean Requiem dream

In memoriam N. S., who created pictures of the ocean depths.

Under the waves … We walked, not swam,
Walked down, through shimmering grey halls
Hung with green clouds like mermaid tails,
Past twirled and curling alcoves, crammed
With sounds of conch and waterfalls,
And the slow moan of distant whales.

Down the long slopes, down, down, we trudged.
The caves opened to greet us. Deep
Spirals of booming chant. Strange eyes,
Ancient as ooze, peered from the sludge.
We passed the record depth of sleep,
And reached the bottom from which dreams rise:

White stones gleaming in pearl-grey light.
White bones twisting themselves to new
Fabulous beasts of horn and echo
Locked in some immemorial fight …
We walked on slowly … Then, askew,
Straddling the jagged floor, that flicker

Of poison tongue, that rasp of jaws,
Black warty skin, and mould-warped scales,
The nightmare demon blocked our way.
Caught in the crack of one of its claws
Was a thing like the song of whales
Curving in rainbows far away,

A brightness and a vanishing ...
Was this the pearl of price we dreamt
We'd glimpse one day? Our gaze buckled,
Snapped ... The nightmare sludge-darkness wings
Covered our vision, monster feet stamped
Out every gleam, and a huge force pulled

Us back, up from the depths, and hurled
Us out on a stranger shore ... But while
We dragged our bruised legs up the shingle —
That white stone ... ? No, it's not *the* pearl ...
Though a whalesong echo seems to dangle
Over *a* pearl, gone into exile.

Stone Circle and Burial Mound

Near the stone circle of Avebury is the Kennet Long Barrow. In the inner room of the burial chamber it is usual to find little offerings of flowers or wheat left on the stones, tokens offered to a Neolithic grave by 21st century people.

Burial mound and standing stones;
Vastness of green stretches away
Into a distance of frozen mist.
Dream! Listen for ghosts. Could a scrap of bone's
Mutter through slumber tease us to play
Games learnt from their skeleton forest

Where giants and dwarves loom like shadows
Sliding between the stones, and laughter
From royal spectres echoes on the hills
In answer to the dead kings' burial barrows?
Are the words clear? They're spoken softer
Than ladybird rustle on daisy petals.

Here is a home, but not for us.
We're given glimpses, a whisper, a scent …
Will it lodge under memory,
Forgotten, unnoticed, until some loss,
Some strange pain, knocks a tiny dent,
A crack in consciousness, and we,

Spinning round .. round .. time's back entrance,
Become for this immeasurable minute
The burial mound, and the dead within it,
As the standing stones begin their dance?

Icarus

"As if seized, floating, on air not water,
Up through the taste of the fear of height,
Through spikes of dazzle, up into an outer
Atmosphere of uncluttered light,

"Whose radiance lifts the word-clogged mind
Through a hungry storm-cloud's fragrant drifting
Over the debris left behind
For worm desires to nibble, for sifting

"Fingers to rummage .. Oh, higher, higher,
The waking dream, the painless pain,
The perfect tension of frost and fire,
Above the bickerings of praise and blame,

Till, piercing a sheath of golden space,
Everything's glimpsed as one, in one
Split vision of instantaneousness
Far brighter than the brightest sun."

Scallop

"Scallop", a memorial to Benjamin Britten on Aldeburgh beach, over which
children climb and play: Maggi Hambling's 4-metre-high steel sculpture of a
broken scallop shell inspired by watching fireworks as a child.

She stands on the sea's knife-edge and catches
The moment between .. life and death —
A sculpted shell, a breaking wave.
The children climb on top of her crashings,
Still steel which mimics the motionless
Nano-second before the dive

Of a million tons' exploding foam.
The crowds of kiddies and zimmer-frame
Ancients, beginning or bringing to conclusion
Man's five minute life-span — their eyes roam
Through momentary wave pictures to tame
The sea's wild beasts ... She captures confusion,

And, while celebrating it, she changes
It into a glimpse between the tick
Of seconds, glimpse of shimmering pause
In the sea's music, glimpse of death's lunges
At life, and tries to split the thick
Cloud of that blackness when the jaws

Of the killer monster open. She knows
Nothing, paints nothing, but time does stop.
A scallop shell in her rough hands
Calloused from carving impertinent stone,
Grows to a wave of steel, whose top
Splinters for us in foam, and lands

At our feet, lies like a muddy dog
Resting after the chase, and then
Slinks back into the unknown wildness.
Stand, as if balanced on unsteady logs,
On the edge of life and death, and end,
Beginning ... Child's firework happiness ...

The Lying-still Walk

Nan Shepherd, in The Living Mountain describes walking in the Cairngorms
without climbing the summits. The importance of touch — thinking
through touch.

> *"The hands have an infinity of pleasure in them. The feel of things, textures,
> surfaces, rough things like cones and bark, smooth things like stalks and
> feathers and pebbles rounded by water, the teasing of gossamers ... the
> scratchings of lichen. The warmth of the sun, the sting of hail, the blunt blow
> of tumbling water, the flow of wind — nothing that I can touch or that touches
> me but has its own identity for the hand as much as for the eye."*

A woman lying on a granite slab;
White-haired and weather-whipped, in grey
Peat-stained anorak, fell boots, her trousers
The blurred colours of moorland drab.
Her eyes, lifted to the scudding sky,
Are shut. Her hands — fists opening, closing ...

Not dead, not asleep. Some waking dream?
Only her hands are active. She stretches:
Spread palms lie flat on the granite. Her eyes,
Opening so slowly, the source of a stream
Seeping through heather and moss, she reaches
Out, touches the bent, rolls on to her side,

Feeling ... Her fingers, like rivulets,
Flow over her slab, her boulders, her heather,
Her peaty soil, for she herself
Is feeder tarn from which streams, bred
In her cold depths, gush hither and thither
Over the stony flesh of the fell.

Her feathery touch hops like a bird —
Pipit? Stonechat? Peewit? — The moss
Answers her moth-brittle fingering
With whispers of smell — damp-breathing earth,
Smouldering odours of peat, rough grass
Chewed by the sheep. She moves her tongue

Over her lips, then slowly, slowly —
Supreme muscle control — she lifts
Herself like sunrise, sits, looks down
Her heather slope, her forested valley,
Breathing horizons of moors. "What a gift"
Thought prompts "it is to have a crown

"Of clouds to wear, so that my head
Switches off thinking brain, becomes
A footstep floating over this hill,
This heather, this moss, this wind-stroked bent.
Lying on granite I hear the earth's drums.
Walking should include lying still."

Agoraphobia

David Jones served as an incompetent private in the First World War, including the battle of the Somme. *In Parenthesis* was his account of his experiences in the trenches, which he turned into powerful myth. The war left him psychically wrecked, and his final accommodation was one room in a Harrow nursing home. To go to the toilet required a walk of about a hundred feet. Next to the toilet was a French door, opening on a fine view over London. Though physically capable of stepping outside to enjoy the view, he never ever did so.

As well as painting the Arthurian legends, he did a series of views looking through windows.

I, who am bound to my chair by a chain
Steel-stronger and lighter than spider web,
A cord spun from my nerves, my mind,
Sit at my window. I feel no pain.
The cord advises me: "Take one step
Outside this room, and you'll go blind.

"Sit at the window here, and look
At the trees, the grass, the wings of the birds,
The moths clung to the glass, the space
Which flows like rivers over rocks
Into deep lakes. Be thankful the cord's
Binding so tight. Up from this place

"Your eyes, your soul, your imagination,
Can fly unchecked. This window is not
Panels of glass forming a wall
To shut you in. This window, spatial
Anomaly, lets you hurtle out,
And soar, falcon, over waterfall,

"Leaving this garden far below.
Through this entrance, and this alone,
You'll find Essyllt, be her Tristan,
Drink from the sacred cup, and know
Merlin's wisdom, the sword in the stone,
And, through this opening, how Earth began."

The shell-shocked man clutched his chair-arms.
Head sunk on chest, he seemed to be sleeping.
We hoped he would stay free from harm
In agoraphobia's watchful keeping.

Collapsing Babel

An old writer, aware of his approaching death, is clearing clutter, including books;
he dreams about the Tower of Babel; for him now, even language itself is turning
to clutter.

The word-tower, having been sentenced,
Cracks, shreds like fabric — strips of torn cloud
Drop on us. We, knocked backwards, lurch,
Stagger, and fall, as the sky, bent,
Hail-hammered, splinters, with screeching sounds
Of steel ripped jagged, while blocks of scorched

Ambition destruct to crumbling flakes
Which lie like stumble-stones, block paths
Leading away from the spire of height.
The crowd's proud anthem? Blown to squeaks,
Twitterings, beetle-scratch; their oaths,
Boasts — pebble-rattle, but magnified

A million times. The lunatic clatter
Of oratory crashing like smashed walls,
And walls collapsing as people are toppled
By torrents of storm able to rattle
Mile-high edifices like marbles
In a child's pocket … Our ears, crippled

By such volcano assaults of noise
Are held like babies in arms by dark
Clutches of silence, which seem to guide
Us down blind lanes through gaps in the sky's
Devastation. Here there's no murk
From smoke explosion, no after-the-raid

Dirt and destruction scatter of wreckage.
Only the silence of pure absence …
Our crippled ears begin to listen,
Our wounded eyes to see. Our baggage
Loaded with language, our brand-new tents
Of paragraph and phrase, our glistening

New kitchen utensils of metaphor,
Periphrasis, and simile,
Have all been swept away like dust
Under the charge of galloping storm.
Where is the blast-scorched tower? We
No longer need know. For now we must

Walk through absence, wrapped in its dark,
Wait till its silence chooses to speak.
And though such waiting will be bleak work —
Our noises have shrunk us, made us weak —
Wait, smaller than dormice-ghosts, for night's
Aeons of blindness to heal our sight.

Butterfly Terror

*Denn das Schöne ist nichts
als des Schrecklichen Anfang, den wir noch grade ertragen,
und wir bewundern es so, weil es gelassen verschmäht,
uns zu zerstören.* Rainer Maria Rilke, *from **Duino Elegies 1***

For Beauty's nothing
But beginning of Terror we're still just able to bear,
And why we adore it so is because it serenely
Disdains to destroy us. Translated by J.B.Leishman & Stephen Spender

The terror, fragile as butterfly
Wings in heat-haze, or morning mist
Lifting kingcups into a sky
Frothy with pollen, approached, and kissed

Me gently once on the cheek, and once
Full on the lips, then walked away.
Some words fluttered past — "I like puns.
I can't pronounce Welsh ells. The play's

"About to start. Goodbye." I shrank
To beetle size. "That's better. Now
You're nearer terra firma." I sank
Into the soil. "Earth does allow

"You to vanish." Why did these words
Keep coming, when she'd drifted a long
Way off by now? Each speck of dirt
Loomed over me like a crag. Like song

Echoes, her words kept wafting round
My shrinking. Earth. Earth — terra. Fear —
Terror. Though she had not returned,
Terror was everywhere, the sheer

Beauty of terror, soft as a moth,
A blown petal. "Will you come back?"
I called to the silence, and like a puff
Of wind, the silence answered. My back

Snapped, and so, beetle-squashed, I lay
In the path where terror's children play.

Espaces Infinis
"Le silence éternel de ces espaces infinis m'effraie." Blaise Pascal

The savagery of space: these stars
Bombarding blackness till their light's
Exploding missile points are spears
Into the void growing inside

Our emptying minds. Both light and dark
Seem here only to crush, tear, shred,
Us into the nothing — not one mark
Of our existence, not even dead

Dust-motes blown down infinity
To terrify us with outer space …
There's no need for the immensity
Of star-distance black nothingness,

Since nothingness is what we are,
And always have been, always will
Be, while these quite indifferent stars,
Spinning endlessly past us, spill
Their useless light from so .. so .. far …

Unconquered Love

from Sophocles' *Antigone*, lines 781 — 802

Creon has sentenced his niece Antigone to death for disobeying his edict. His son, Haemon, in love with Antigone, has been pleading with his father to spare her. Creon obstinately refuses; it is clear Haemon will do something terrible. This dance of love's power follows, after which the guards enter, escorting Antigone to her death by being walled up in a cave.

An isometric translation, preserving the musical pattern of the Greek, so that it could be set to the same tune as the original.

Unconquered love, toppling estates,
Unconquered love, slackening armies.
As soft as a dream of kissing
The cheek of a virgin sleeping,
You stride across oceans, or strike
Shepherds in small, far, huts.
No power, even immortal, can escape you.
No man with his life of moments.
Love, you can crack your mansions.

You tempt the good, baffle the wise,
And drag the just down to injustice.
This quarrel of son with father
Is passion at war with kinship.
Who'll fight a clear yes in the eyes
Opening a girl's soft bed?
Love, sex, passion, what force, depths, elementals!
Love, sex, what a game, what battles!
Love, what a god unconquered!

Genesis Woman

Last night, I'm making a world from fluff,
Lark-song, and a lizard's discarded tail,
When a woman shouted "You've caused enough
Trouble already. God's female,

"And worlds can't be created by men."
She was red-hot, a lava flow
Of rock-melt, fire, and sulphur. "When
You can bear heat like this, then go

"Out into space, creating" she sneered.
"The world I'm making's very small"
I stammered. "Oh you're worse than I'd feared"
She boomed — "the talent of a brick wall.

"Men can do nothing. They can't even
Become women without surgery,
While women can easily become men.
Penises? Piece of cake." Quickly

She reached up on to a dusty shelf,
Fumbled, grabbed, some male private parts,
And carelessly fixed them on to herself,
Over her knickers. "Women make art.

"Men are bogged down with fighting and sex.
You create worlds? Ridiculous.
All you create is rubbish and wrecks.
How dare you try to be gods like us!"

Decent chap, Robin

Florid complexion, forty-two,
Six feet, and fourteen stone, he hunts,
Plays polo, tennis, loves opera,
Passably hums some aria tunes,
Looks as you'd imagine Mozart's Count
Almaviva, collects china,

Runs his own merchant bank, divorced,
Sometimes plays blackjack Friday nights,
Sometimes picks up a high-class tart,
Tells jokes — impeccable timing, of course.
He knows exactly how to excite
Women, but also studies the art

Of friendship with men. "Ruthless, but fair,"
"Good for a laugh, but has to win,"
"Keep him on your side," and comments
Like that. He has causes, still cares
For his ex-wife — an alchy in
Some clinic or other ... Robin has spent

A fortune on his boys' education.
He's no Gestapo, no SS.
He'd slaughter Nazis, not Jews. He likes
People, dogs, horses. Experimentation
On living creatures? Never, unless
Essential for saving human life.

Decent man, Robin ... I watched him buy
His new lover a leopard-skin coat.
Nude, they could model for Mars and Venus.
Robin knows how those leopards die:
For a flawless skin you kill the cat
With a red-hot poker up its anus.

The Silk

for Keith and Julie who did not have 500 guineas, let alone the £10,000.

"Flourishing like bay trees — " he said
"The wicked!" Chuckling, he poured a second
Large measure of whisky. Overweight,
But still handsome. A zappy red
Tie, and a Savile Row suit we reckoned
Cost several hundred pounds. Our fate

Depended on his judgement. "We must
Make sure" he went on "that this time
The good flourish. I'll take your case."
He poured himself a third full glass,
Sipped generously. "It should be a crime,
What they did to you." His Silk face —

Perfect except for boozer veins —
Projected 'Saviour!' "Give me three days
To read the papers. I'll contact you.
Meanwhile, perhaps, a small .. against
Current expenses .. sorry to raise
The matter, but .. hrrmph .. becomes due ... "

His language turned precise again.
His fee for our ten minutes was
Five hundred guineas. If he took
The case, he'd do it for under ten ..
Thousand pounds, being generous.
Five hundred guineas — but we're broke.
So: exit down his marble steps,
Un-umbrellaed, into the drizzle drips ...

We hear Silk's been engaged by the crook.

Liberation

When the soldiers came, we were asleep ...
In the dark hour just before dawn —
Crashes. The panic of kicked-in doors,
The clatter of wheel-rattle in our street.
Then we heard shouts: "Liberation!
We're here to rescue you, restore

"The rightful government. Wake up,
Brothers and sisters! Learn to be free
Again." And now tinges of grey
Dawn half-light slowly seeming to rub
Itself against the shadowy trees
And buildings. Old women started to pray,

Gabbling hurriedly, mumbling toothless,
Like dry mouths masticating stale bread.
Grannies know only too well the meaning
Of that word, commandeered by ruthless
Leaders — Yes. "Liberated" means dead
For half the people, while the remaining

Half learn obediently how to shout new
Slogans with slavishly assumed
Adoration for the conquerors.
We try to sidle away. A few
Of us, cowed ghosts in the threatening gloom,
Slink from confronting skilled murderers

Hard at work: officers' words of command
Swamped by the screams of victims. We
Make for the tunnel — no point in trying
To save the old woman at prayers, her hands
Caught in a ray of sunrise. She,
Calm, hardly aware, her daughter crying,

Both killed so easily, the soldier
Hardly checking his stride. Now. Quick.
Into the tunnel. Puddles and mud.
A stumbling floor strewn with large boulders
And dangerous holes. We have two sick
Children to carry. Hurry. The wood

At the tunnel's end, ancient forest.
Tangles of thicket thorn-traps. Hills
Make it easy to lose all sense
Of orientation. No, we can't rest
Till we're well hidden. Hope the thorns will
Spring back and hide our path, prevent

Soldiers from guessing our route. Let's find
Our way through, down to the sea, and then
A new life somewhere very far
From our .. liberated country — mind,
That creeper's poisonous. Those men,
Those killers, truly believe they are

Freeing this nation from slavery
By forcing corpses to cheer for liberty.

The Noble Victory

"Wicked, wicked, children, to throw stones at the kind tanks liberating you."

Us? Fumbling rush to reach the corner,
Slip round, and flatten against the wall.
Them? Grinding scrunch of unoiled wheels,
Rattling tank-track thunder. Us? Mourners
Like rivers in flood diverted, a whole
Smashed city of rubble, wounds, and squealing,

Huddled in panic. Them? Down wrecked streets
Conquering heroes ride. Their flags
Proclaim devotion to liberty, peace,
Good government. Having defeated
Our wobbly crowd of weeping hags
And toddlers, they'll herd us boy beasts,

Who dared throw stones at their jet planes
And airborne missiles, into neat camps
Decorated with new barbed wire.
First we're scrubbed down .. with shit; then games:
Guards playing football with our heads, stamp
On each of us in turn. Then prayers:

Face down in the dirt, intone ten times:
"We're murderers, we're terrorists,
We kill civilians," on the hour;
Afterwards be charged with war crimes.
Them? Conquering army's missile fist —
Which pulped a million children, tore

A population into strips
Of rag — opening in smart salute.
Good guys, who've shown just how to whip
Us bad guys, trampling us with polished boots.

The Non-dom City Trader

Sitting at ease in a tower of glass,
His smile flows over cities like oil,
Till every building and every street
Dissolves in a wash of thinglessness,
While every inhabitant, now soiled
With stains of failure and fumbled defeat,

Quietly chokes in the clinging ooze.
High in his glass room, his pale, rich,
Fingers manipulate vast wealth's
Encrypted digits. Bank-draft shoes
Slide across soft skin carpet which
Once wrapped the body of a child — himself.

Cities, countries, and continents,
Forests and oceans, valleys and hills,
Carpenters, lovers, the old, the young,
Like starving tiny birds — tits, wrens,
Goldcrests — plop out of a sky frost-filled
Lethal, and vaporise. His tongue

Slobbers wetly over fat zeros
Multiplying on his barren screen —
Wealth which reaps, builds, makes, heals, nothing
But lines of noughts. Non-person Nero,
Destroying Rome without fire, he's
Non-dom, the City's Fiddler King.

Outside Brixton Tube Station

stands a man in a golden robe, doing nothing all day.

Tall handsome black, in golden robes
And turban, always spotless-clean.
African? Yes. Nigerian?
Benin? Some prince of treasure-trove
Tropical legend whose prophecies mean
He must be — he is — the Chosen One?

He walks like song, looks down his nose
At briefcase-suits, shorts and bum-bags,
Torn jeans, ex-army jump-jackets,
Scuffed trainers — mine with holes in the toes —
All of us, trendy, drab, in rags,
School-kid satchels, tramps laying bets,

Arthur Daleys selling duff watches,
Socks, calculators, nice little earners
Fallen off lorries; the wino who sits
Downing the equivalent of ten scotches
As he heats his guts to a humming furnace
Of lager-cider cocktail with splits

Of wine in Lloyds Bank doorway. Prince,
In your gold robes and turban, why
D'you stand all day by Brixton tube
Station? And who pays your rent, since
You can't possibly work? Your dry-
Cleaning bill must be loan-shark huge

With the gloop-gunge-yuck muck calling itself
Air in traffic-blocked Brixton Road.
And aren't you hot this August day,
Temperature ninety? You've nothing to sell,
Except your beauty. You look so proud,
So royal, I doubt even crack-crazed,

Dope-vacuumed-brainless, Brixton braves
Would dare approach you — or have the price
To kiss your hand. There's always a preacher
Or two here, yelling how de Lord saves
Us all from sin, near-losing his voice.
But you're no over-the-truck-roar screecher.

You never talk. You simply stand,
Or stroll slowly in your gold robes,
Like magi in ancient pictures, or wizards
From fairy-tales. Robes aptly designed
For you, unique; we and our clothes
Are dust-motes; you're our sun, new-risen.

I daren't ask, but I'd love to know your business.

PC Ted Scroggins RIP

A fat copper on a slow bicycle.

Even for a copper, he had huge feet;
He'd rumble up fire-escape stairs
Like a wheelie-bin. What a loud laugh:
A thunderstorm-cloud's bass-drum beat
With rainbow cymbals. Ted, the bear
Who loved honey, could be a giraffe

Reaching up into lofts for secret
Forgotten oddments. Then he'd tell
Stories, or whistle blades of dry grass.
He'd pick up knick-knacks . " 'Ere .. take it"
He'd murmur — armadillo shell,
Nelson's Victory carved in a glass

Bottle, pipe owned by a famous actor
Of the last century — these gifts
Saved from bulldozers. Ted's voice could boom,
Swoop cackling like a pterodactyl,
But also tiptoe through cupboards and lofts
Like tiny mice. An African drum

He'd kept for himself. Cannibal rhythms —
He beat them out till our ears tingled.
"Copper on the beat!" — his joke. Never passed
Sergeant's exam. Beat copper, not driven
By any ambition. His eyes would crinkle
In a slow smile: "I always came last

"In the races or the exams at school".
He went to rescue a wounded wife,
Battered by hubby. "Please sir" — Ted trying
To say "Let's have a talk. Please cool
Down, sir." Hubby grabs kitchen knife —
Into Ted's guts .. wife starts crying

"You've killed him". Exclamation mark
Death. Life blotted out. No, there'll be no
Obituary in the national press,
Mention on telly. Bench in the park
With a brass plaque we've ordered, to show
How much we thought of him. "The best

Copper in Brixton — PC Ted
Scroggins" was what the inscription said.

Chippenham Station Cleaner

The cleaner's remarks were exactly as quoted here.

Ex-con perhaps? A rag-soggy-
with-dirty-water kind of man,
The station cleaner: minute bits
Of rubbish and dust, so, so slowly
Brushed into his battered, rusty pan
Stained with the smell of stale toilets.

Slow-motion trudge, near stationary,
He sweeps a few dog-ends. The real
Ingrained dirt, now pressed into the floor,
As though glazed onto the tiles, filthy —
So filthy it's as if clean, normal —
His dingy routine lets him ignore.

Dingy routine, always the same —
Round booking-hall anti-clockwise
In slinking invisibility,
Past ticket-machine where people claim
Their pre-paid tickets. A man arrives
With wife and luggage in great hurry.

The booking hall is empty. But
The station cleaner has his routine:
At this moment he's due to sweep
Round ticket machine: Passenger, mind out;
Step back; I'm sweeping. I have to clean
This fraction of floor .. *Now!* I must keep

To the predetermined movement plan,
Me, Field Marshal of a dog-end world —
Or thoughts like that. What he said was
"Can't you see I'm .. cleaning here. Stand
Aside." The wife abruptly told
Him not to be so rude: "Get lost.

"We're in a hurry." Cleaner's reply?
"You're ignorant!" His life's routine
As dog-end-scooping-up machine
Rudeness alone can dignify.

In a Glasgow Back Street

Having learnt to carry wilderness
In hands, or eyes, or ears,
While kicking beer-cans into clogged gutters,
Stepping over squashed chips and chewed chicken-bones,
Nostrils clogged with diesel fumes,
Ears scorched by police sirens,
His soul lifted out of his dwindling body,
Soared and swooped falcon-winged
Through the mauve light of heather moorland.

So when the crowd of pub-closing-timers
Carelessly booted his dwindling body
Like a beer-can into the gutter,
He had already vacated it as inadequate premises …

The Erratic Professor

Scrawny and shabby — a tangle of rope-
ends-coming-undone sort of man
With a wambling walk. Bald head, stray hairs
Dribbling down shoulders, grey, greasy. Like apes
Confined to their zoo-cage prison —
Purposeless pacing here and there —

His lectures were like a pile of notes
On backs of envelopes, odd scraps
Of crumpled wrapping strewn on floors
Never hoovered. They blew about
From ancient Crete, to the "Polish chaps
Fighting the Battle of Britain", to the door

Of the Florence duomo, to harnessing
Nuclear fusion as electric power.
Use his lectures for passing exams?
Certain failure. He seemed to fling
Fragments of sticky stardust at your
Neat white shirt-front notes, or chuck jam

Up in the air for you to catch
On stale bread slices. The council of dons
Kept trying to ban his lectures. Crowds
Of students flocked to listen, to snatch
Illuminations fluttering down
From a summer sky whose lark-song shouted

Praises for the eccentricity
Of human nature. He had no great
Theory of history, only muddles,
Cock-ups. His world? Bomb-blasted cities
In which strange flowers bloom in the grates
Of fireplaces left standing in rubble

Where there had once been walls. He simply
Spoke his thoughts out aloud. He took
No notice of syllabus. His home
Was books and books and books and empty
Bottles and dust. No door had a lock.
Cobwebs festooned his dank bedroom.

He never published. What would be left
Of him once he had died? Nothing?
Nothing except weird memories
To appear like unexpected gifts
In the minds of ex-students, aging
In diverse jobs, diverse countries:

Boys, girls, who'd swapped a commendation
By syllabus — for inspiration.

Poet as Vandal

Alexander Pope did precisely as the poem describes.

Designing gardens is an occupation
Most suitable for poets. Cultivation
Whether of rose, or cabbage, soothes the nagging
Of unformed phrases, mutes the foolish bragging
Of talentless rivals. Spread mulch! What about
Building a grotto? Grottos can give clout
To any garden. That, at least, is what
Pope — Alexander Pope — thought: "Yes! Why not
Tunnel under the road, thus linking my
Garden with my lawn by the Thames, so I
Can step out from my grotto on a view
Of light and water, swans and herons too.
Not a mere tunnel, though. A grotto cave,
Offering twilight mysteries you'll brave
With trembling candles held aloft. What? Mere
Statues which other grottos boast? No. Here
You shall find Nature's sculpture, none of Man's."
Pope dreamt down deeper while he drew his plans.
His inspiration came from Wookey Hole: —
Stalactites, stalagmites — caverns with soul:
Rain leaking through the limestone, drip, drip, drop,
Growing an inch a century, till, plop
By plop, pimples on the cave floor become
Statues of monsters, winking witches, dumb
Screamers and deaf singers — tall stalagmites,
While ceiling drips grow pterodactyls, flights
Of falcons, eagles, angels — stalactites.
Nature's water-carved statues aren't for sale,
Though. Pope: "I won't suffer my vision to fail,"
Thinks "Army!" "Platoon, quick march!" he orders, leads
Soldiers down Wookey Hole. Now for great deeds
Of military valour such as will quite soon

Win Britain empires. Pope yells out "Platoon!
Load muskets! Aim! Fire!" But what enemy
Falls wounded, broken? Limestone statuary
Carved by Dame Nature over centuries.
Pope's grotto sculpture? A unique display.
But Wookey Hole remains damaged today.
So Pope, the scourge of eighteenth century scandal,
Was himself an environmental vandal.

Hi-tech Hazards

He proudly purchased a planet
With atmosphere and life-forms,
In a nearby galaxy.
His spacecraft's robot intelligence
Developed human emotions,
And dropped out on an asteroid.

So he spliced his genes
With those from an oak-tree,
In the hope of living a thousand years.
To his horror, his children
Grew up into dining-room tables.

Then, having cloned himself
Several million times,
He died of mass starvation.

Yvonne's Frog Prince

While stripping wallpaper from her bedroom wall,
Yvonne was assaulted by a horny frog,
Which threw her on to the bed, and balled
Her seventeen times with his huge green cock.

Yvonne, at first, was annoyed and surprised,
But as soon as he'd pulled her panties down,
The touch of his cool green fingers aroused
Her so much that she felt she'd drown

In breath-frothing underwater orgasms.
He eased her through whirlpools. She oozed over lakes,
Drifted down steam-bubble frond-tickly chasms
That squirmed and writhed with shrieking sea-snakes.

After five hours of somersault sex,
As they lay exhausted on the dust-sheeted bed,
The green cock still giving jokey jerks,
Yvonne plucked up her courage and said:

"Tell me: are you a fairy-tale prince?
Why are you having it off with me?
I'm just a housewife with three kids.
I thought one kiss set frog-princes free."

His words croaked out like underwater glugs:
"Spell processor ... prince-print-out ... bugs."

"You're my prince-bint. But we're spawn-pawns
Caught in bond-frond of frog-jig
On a bonk-bank in a time-warp
Where a frigweb of cobspawn
Pokes croaks up your creek.
So, my prick-freak, be frog-fond:
Let us shriek, leak, and stroke-bond,
Till my dong-wand of prince-spunk
Spills dadpoles in your mumspell,
As each frogball scores tadgoals
On our bonk-banged tadspilt sheet."

Yvonne said "Are you telling me I'll never be a princess, and I'm
probably pregnant with a load of tadpoles?"
Then she threw him into the pond. But as he landed in the water,
she looked down and saw that her toes had become webbed, and
her skin was turning green.

The Dance of the Frogs
from Aristophanes' *The Frogs*: lines 209 — 269

In comedy, everything is topsy-turvy. Dionysus — who is also the god Hades — is trying to get into Hades, by 'rowing' across the lake of Hades in a caricature of the ship-car in which the Dionysus statue was carried in the Dionysiac festival procession. This is a boat on wheels; the actor's feet come through the bottom of the boat so he can walk it across the orchéstra floor. The Frogs are ghosts of the worshippers of Dionysus, the worshippers who pull the ship-car. The singing — croaking — contest between Dionysus and the Frog Chorus is choreographed as a kind of tug-of-war, with the frogs pulling his boat, but pulling it in the wrong direction. Finally Dionysus out-screeches the frogs, and gets across the lake. There he is met by his servant who has simply walked round, since, in comedy, everything is topsy-turvy.

An isometric translation, preserving the musical pattern of the Greek, so that it could be set to the same tune as the original.

CHORUS OF FROGS
Brekekekex koahx koahx.
Brekekekex koahx koahx.
We are the pond-bogside kids.
So blow that horn. We've arrived
Hymn-singing. How d'you like this tune? Some rhythm!
Koahx koahx.
Once — oh what a beat we had.
We sang for the Lord of Life
Bogside Dionysus' shrine,
Smashed as a blessed pitcher
Pouring the blessed liquor,
We'd rave to the shrine, and we were .. alive .. people.
Brekekekex koahx koahx.

DIONYSUS
At this with pain I start to gasp.
Koahx koahx
I've got a sore arse.
But I suppose you couldn't care less.

CHORUS OF FROGS
Brekekekex koahx koahx.

DIONYSUS
To hell with you and your koahx.
You're nothing but — koahx koahx.

CHORUS OF FROGS
Serve you right for interfering.
We are beloved by all music-loving spirits.
Demon of the hoof-dance with his whistle-winds a-blowing —
As for the Lord of golden harp — how they adore me ...
There is a musical instrument industry
Out of the bamboo stems from ponds.

DIONYSUS
And I've got blisters on my — oh!
My arse is sweating ever so.
And soon it will pop up and go —

CHORUS OF FROGS
Brekekekex koahx koahx.

DIONYSUS
My dear musicians, do stop.
Less brio!

CHORUS OF FROGS
Certainly not!
We shall croak as we can croak
All day long in sunny summer,
Leaping through the rushes and sedges,
Leaping high, croaking for pleasure,
Plenty of plunge-plopping melody.
Rainy days we still go dancing —
Easy to shelter under water —
There we play our double forte
Pondbubble-an'-splatsplashmachine.

DIONYSUS
Brekekekex koahx koahx.
I'll play your tune, take it from you.

CHORUS OF FROGS
That's a dreadful noise you're making.

DIONYSUS
Nothing to the noise when I start breaking.
Stop, or I shall split in two.

CHORUS OF FROGS
Brekekekex koahx koahx.

DIONYSUS
Oh go to hell. I couldn't care less.

CHORUS OF FROGS
Yes, and we shall croak crescendo
Long as our throat can keep wide open
All the day from dawn to dusk.

DIONYSUS
Brekekekex koahx koahx.
You'll never get away with this.

CHORUS OF FROGS
Nor will your voice top me either.

DIONYSUS
Nor will you top my reprise.
Never ever. For I'll crescendo
Even if it takes all day.
Brekekekex koahx koahx.
Till I, sforzando, diminuendo your koahx.
Brekekekex koahx koahx.
I thought I stood a fair chance of stopping your koahx.

The Dalai Lama Waxwork

Madam Tussauds: poster ad shows 2 waxworks — Dalai Lama and .. not him ?

Fame is the spur that the clear spirit doth raise
(That last infirmity of noble mind)
To scorn delights and live laborious days.
John Milton, *Lycidas* lines 70 - 72

Is fame his spur? How his clear spirit prays,
Scorning delights, living laborious days.
Brought up in the mountain winds of bleak Tibet
Without too much delight in the food he ate,
The mattress he slept on, the call to rise
Well before dawn, his fists pummelling his eyes.
Laborious days toughened by meditation
While mountain-trudging through his ravaged nation.
Then the flight — up the glaciers, through crevasses,
Traversing snow-slopes, to the cold high passes.
Then exile in India, now permanent,
All to escape from life-imprisonment
Muzzled by Chinese thugs and murderers,
While his Tibet's razed by Red monk-killers.
Is fame his spur? I doubt it. To maintain
Buddhism, till his staunch Tibetans regain
Tibet, to encourage his bullied and scattered
Followers to hold on: that is what mattered
To him, I guess, not the trappings of fame.

But — Dalai Lama — the media knows his name.
He's a celeb of sorts. Britain applauds
Him — put his waxwork in Madam Tussauds.
Tussauds has poster-ads stuck up round London.
But even our star-crazed media might be stunned on
Seeing the Dalai Lama, symbol of peace,
Placed, right of centre, next to one of these
TV celebs, fashionable like fast
Food — someone called Titchmarsh, whose fame will last
Only until he blunts his new hedge-clippers —
A TV gardener who writes bodice-rippers.

Hollywood History

Hollywod's devotion to historical accuracy is well-known, and exhibited most emphatically in movies about the Second World War such as the one where it is Americans who capture Enigma, the German code machine, or in their version of the Battle of Britain, won more or less single-handed by Tom Hanks, Spitfire pilot.

God bless America, land of the free,
Downing dictators, largessing liberty
Even to people who don't appreciate
Uncle Sam's rejig of their nation state.
Just as in Star Trek, when brave Captain Kirk
Beams down on planets, and Spock gets to work
With his computers, Yank technology
And Can-do solves all problems instantly.
Cowardly Japs caught Uncle Sam pants down
In Pearl Harbour, bombed warships, factories, town.
But Uncle Sam's production-lines were speeded
Up till they spat out all the gear he needed —
Tanks, planes, guns, atom bombs, as the G.I.s
Spread out across the world zapping bad guys.
While Limey airmen slunk into air-raid shelters,
And Messerschmidts chased Spitfires helter-skelter,
The Battle of Britain was — hold your breath — won,
Against all odds, all on his own, by one
Pilot, the champion top-gun of the Yanks,
Luftwaffe's scourge, Squadron Leader Tom Hanks.
With Europe still flattened by Nazi boots,
A West Point drop-out leading raw recruits —
Monty Montgomery, raised in Iowa —
A true son of mid-west America —
Saved Egypt from Rommel's panzer campaign,
Winning the victory of Alamein.

On Yankee know-how you can put reliance.
Americans are the world-leaders in science.
Physicists like little Mike Faraday
From Ashland Wisconsin, daring to play
With magnets, wires — poof! — electricity!
Or Chuck Darwin, known for his eccentricity
In Elk, Kansas, who solved the human genome
Studying tortoises in his kiddy tree-home.
Zak Newton too, who kept an apple orchard
In Kellog, Idaho, and sometimes tortured
Wasps for wrecking his fruit, was once caught napping.
Apple falls on his head. Zak jumps up, clapping,
Shouts "Got it! Gravity! The universe
Powered by gravity!" His bent old nurse
Smiles at him. "Isaac, Isaac, you're so funny.
Gravity, schmavity! Vill it make money?"
Bill Shakespeare, who used to work pumping gas
In Androscoggin, Maine, upped, hauled his ass
To Hollywood, started by writing gags
For sit-coms, then teams up with those bright fags,
And runs an all-guys company for some years,
Has hits on HBO, then disappears,
Leaves Hollywood, goes in for real estate
In Stratford, England, drinks, cokes, puts on weight,
While agents cheat him of his royalties,
So, though his ratings soar, his own life is
A proper mess. What about Magna Carta?
Without Americans — zilch. A non-starter.

Those Limey barons ass-licking King John.
Sir Mel de Gibson cries "Chaps, that's not on,"
Frog-marches in the King, whips out a pen,
"Sign, Johnny," till John signs the charter, then
Flees in a panic. His carriage goes splosh,
Turns over, drops his laundry in the Wash.
Handsome Sir Mel reformed the feudal system,
While peasant lasses greedily French-kissed him.
Thus Uncle Sams have, throughout history,
Worked for world progress, science, liberty,
Above all, movies, which convey the truth
And nothing but the truth, to the world's youth,
Reminding us, that there are always yet
More facts to learn. By the way, don't forget
How Chris Columbo, born in Omaha,
By missing his way discovered America.

The Flabbergasted Hippopotamus

Lists of favourites are fashionable ways of filling spare space in magazines: 100 best movies, holidays, 10 best descriptions of earthquakes in a novel, etc. One such list claimed to be that of the British people's favourite words, including such obvious choices as flip-flop, lollipop, fuselage, gazebo. This poem is composed solely of those favourite words. For those interested the complete list is printed below.

Provided
A blue sunflower, a gothic coconut,
And a flabbergasted hippopotamus,
Can play peekaboo under an umbrella,
Mother, with a smile,
Will set out for her hen night — zing!
Passion will blossom for a hilarious moment,
A sophisticated renaissance of serendipity.
Rainbow butterflies, loquacious bumblebees,
Kangaroos in flip-flops,
Will fill the galaxy with gazebos.
"Our destiny is Liberty" Mother will giggle,
"Cherish your bananas",
As an explosion of sunshine
Blows the fuselage to smithereens,
An extravaganza of twinkling bubbles.
"Enthusiasm may be fantastic"
Hiccups Mother. "But peace
Is a lollipop the size of a pumpkin."

1 Mother 2 Passion 3 Smile 4 Love 5 Eternity 6 Fantastic 7 Destiny 8 Freedom 9 Liberty 10 Tranquility 11 Peace 12 Blossom 13 Sunshine 14 Sweetheart 15 Gorgeous 16 Cherish 17 Enthusiasm 18 Hope 19 Grace 20 Rainbow 21 Blue 22 Sunflower 23 Twinkle 24 Serendipity 25 Bliss 26 Lullaby 27 Sophisticated 28 Renaissance 29 Cute 30 Cosy 31 Butterfly 32 Galaxy 33 Hilarious 34 Moment 35 Extravaganza 36 Aqua 37 Sentiment 38 Cosmopolitan 39 Bubble 40 Pumpkin 41 Banana 42 Lollipop 43 If 44 Bumblebee 45 Giggle 46 Paradox 47 Delicacy 48 Peekaboo 49 Umbrella 50 Kangaroo 51 Flabbergasted 52 Hippopotamus 53 Gothic 54 Coconut 55 Smashing 56 Whoops 57 Tickle 58 Loquacious 59 Flip-flop 60 Smithereens 61 Oi 62 Gazebo 63 Hiccup 64 Hodgepodge 65 Shipshape 66 Explosion 67 Fuselage 68 Zing 69 Gum 70 Hen night

Washing-powder War

Procter and Gamble, manufacturers of Ariel and Bold washing powders, claimed Unilever's New Persil Power rotted boxer shorts; The Independent on Sunday tested this by washing identical boxer shorts 16 times, one pair in Ariel Ultra, and one in Persil Power, and proving there was no difference whatsoever between the two powders. Since this poem resulted from a BBC commission, the company names had to be changed.

The multinational company, Unicrank,
Withdrew one hundred million from the bank,
Drained universities of graduates
With first class honours degrees and first class debts:
Physicists who're at home in Hawking's eerie
Space-time of black holes and Grand Unified Theory,
Biochemists who might — with a stroke of luck —
Culture — yes, life itself, from scraps of muck,
And hired these future Nobels for huge dosh ..
To boost their soap powder. "Our Improved Wash"
They shout "contains A New Accelerator" —
Manganese-something .. or-other — for greater
Penetration into those naughty stains.
They launch a series of wham-bang campaigns.
Housewives are called on by charming young men
Who make them do their wash over again —
Not in "Their Usual Powder" but in ours,
To reveal that our bleach has extra powers,
Though bleach is never mentioned. Only "Brightness,"
And "Whiter than That Other Powder's Whiteness."
Look! Mrs Silly Housewife's clothes are duller,
Washed in Her Usual Powder. Preserve your colour,
Chuck out Brand X. Buy New Parsnip Power only.
Parsnip Power stops your kids from feeling lonely:
Unless boys' shorts gleam like a diadem,
No other boys will want to play with them.

Pocket and Grumble, the rival company
Makes two powders which appear equally
Effective. One of them is called 'Etherial.'
That's best they claim for delicate material
Like silks and lace. For tougher stains use 'Dare.'
Pocket and Grumble, losing market share
To Unicrank, take out huge full-page ads:
"New Parsnip Power is unkind to dads;
New Parsnip Power will rot his boxer shorts."
Unicrank threatens action in the Courts.

A Sunday paper organised a test.
Which of the powders really is the best?
They dropped each pair of boxers in some grime,
Then washed both of them thoroughly sixteen times,
One in Etherial, one in New Parsnip.
Will one emerge faded? Frayed? Will it rip
Easily, being rotten? Will every stitch
Come undone? Here. Have a look. Which is which?
One washed with Parsnip, one Etherial.
The judges' verdict? Both identical.
Each washing-powder company will claim
"Our powder's special." They're all much the same.

Chunnelend

This morning the Prime Minister
Announced the building of the second Channel Tunnel,
And, in order to accommodate the extra traffic generated,
A forty-lane motorway, running in a straight line
From Chunnelend to London,
The latter city now to be renamed Chunnelville,
And, in order to accommodate the extra traffic generated,
A sixty-lane motorway running round Chunnelville,
(Obliterating what used to be called London,)
And, in order that British business in places other than
Chunnelville
Should benefit from better communication with the continent,
A forty-lane motorway, running in a straight line
From Chunnelville to Birmingham
Now renamed Chunnelville Midland,
And, in order to accommodate the extra traffic generated,
A sixty-lane motorway running round Chunnelville Midland,
(Obliterating what used to be called
Birmingham, Coventry, Wolverhampton, Stafford,)
And, in order that British business
In places other than Chunnelville and Chunnelville Midland
Should benefit from better communication with the continent,
A forty-lane motorway, running in a straight line
From Chunnelville Midland to Manchester
Now renamed Chunnelville Northern,
And, in order to accommodate the extra traffic generated,
A sixty-lane motorway running round Chunnelville Northern,
(Obliterating what used to be called
Manchester, Liverpool, Leeds, Sheffield, Bradford, Middlesborough,
York, Darlington, Newcastle,)

And, in order that Scottish business
Should benefit from better communication with the continent,
A forty-lane motorway, running in a straight line
From Chunnelville Northern to Glasgow
Now renamed Chunnelville Caledon,
And, in order to accommodate the extra traffic generated,
A sixty-lane motorway running round Chunnelville Caledon
(Obliterating what used to be called
Glasgow, Edinburgh, Stirling, Aberdeen,
Inverness, and the islands of
Rum, Eigg, Muck, Barra, Uist, Orkney, and Shetland,)
And, as a byproduct of this breath-takingly brilliant
Bridging of the British-continental communications-deficiency,
I am here to offer personally
To each one of you a prospectus
For the share-sale of the millennium:
Our newly privatised atmosphere of pure carbon monoxide.

On Receiving the Queen's Gold Medal for Poetry

What was wrong with my dream
Of walking naked into Buckingham Palace
To receive the Queen's Gold Medal for Poetry,
Lowered eyes demurely observing
Little more than my own bare feet — damn, dirty toenails —
Sliding across the parquet and Aubussons
In the company of morning-dress knife-edge creases
And see-your-face-in-it black Oxfords,
Or the braided blues and greens of sword-clanking number-ones
Digging their heels into priceless carpets as if on parade-grounds,
What was wrong with my dream
Was that when I finally reached the Presence
And lifted figleafless eyes to the Sovereign,
Though she neither ordered my immediate imprisonment
for lèse majesté,
Nor started hans-andersening about my emperor-new
Emerald silks and cramoisie velvets
While modestly claiming preference for her "old duds" —
A Koh-i-noor-brooched Harris-tweed coat and skirt
More suitable for highland grouse-moor than Buck Pal throne-
room,
But, while her dogs were licking between my toes,
She merely asked me whether I liked corgis,
And in an exchange of as-it-were
Over-the-Surbiton-fence doggie-chat,
She forgot to give my medal.

From the *Introduction* by *Alan Brownjohn* to ***Dancing the Impossible: New & Selected Poems*** (in shortened version)

"To read Leo Aylen is to be aware at once of the wide range of interests and backgrounds which serve the endeavours of a resourcefully energetic talent. He had a classical training, and worked originally for the BBC. The classical scholarship is here — though 'scholarship' is too dry a word for his vigorous and sensuous treatment of his themes. His poems show us a passionate and venturesome traveller. And yet the London in which he works as a freelance writer and broadcaster is also rawly present in his verse, a rundown, menacing, metropolis, with many examples of deprived, marginalised humanity.

He derives pleasure from changing the scene and grappling with diverse experience. There is nothing safe and conventional about his poetry. Vigour, enjoyment of playing with the fire of words and images, and an exuberant appetite for rhythms and sounds, are obvious characteristics. Dance, movement, physicality — musicality — are other words that come to mind.

Before 'performance poetry' gained the prominence it now enjoys (the element of performance too often obscuring the weak quality of some of the poems) Aylen was already giving dramatic recitals of his poems in which lively physical presentation enhanced the message of the verse. It also sent listeners on to the poems on the page, where they were as vivid and gripping as they sounded when the poet delivered them from the platform.

Sureness of performance (it goes with necessary yet rare qualities like professionalism) is hugely helped by a sense of timing and structure in what is *being* performed. Aylen's instinct for the suitable length and shape of a poem is very sure.

As a poet he is — would he agree? — unabashedly romantic, wholly unafraid of the bold, or the dangerously vulnerable, statement of feeling. The great American, Robert Lowell, once said that in order to write poetry it was desirable to have 'courage and

a merciful heart.' In his poems of love and other deep emotions, Leo Aylen possesses both of these qualities — and a third: a sense of poetry as an act of celebration, an activity always to be pursued with zest and delight."
Alan Brownjohn

Other books by Leo Aylen

Poetry:
Discontinued Design
I, Odysseus
Sunflower
Return to Zululand
Red Alert: this is a god warning
Jumping-Shoes
Dancing the Impossible: New & Selected Poems

Poetry for Children
The Apples of Youth, *an opera*
Rhymoceros

Non-fiction
Greek Tragedy and the Modern World
Greece for Everyone
The Greek Theater

Acknowledgements

The Day the Grass Came was commended in the **1998 Arvon** prize competition, and published in **The Ring of Words** — The Daily Telegraph 1998 Arvon prize-winners' anthology; *Bloody Refugees* was a **1999 Peterloo** runner-up prize-winner, and published in the Peterloo prize-winners' anthology for that year; *Letter to William* was a **2003 Peterloo** runner-up prize-winner, and published in the Peterloo prize-winners' anthology for that year; *Belfast Incident* was a **2002 Bridport** runner-up prize-winner, and published in the Bridport prize-winners' anthology for that year; *Ocean Requiem Dream, Haida Burial-pole, Stone Circle and Burial Mound*, have been published in **Agenda**; *In a Glasgow Back Street, Espaces Infinis*, have been published in **Acumen**; *An Archaeologist's Intuition, Hi-tech Hazards*, have been published in **Orbis**; *Incident at Llanafan Fawr Powys 1842, Double Funeral, Chosen to Bear Your Child, Yvonne's Frog Prince*, have been published in **Markings**; *Genesis Woman, Butterfly Terror, Glimpsing a Golden Oriole, Tiger Love Affair, So What Is "Love"?* — *Sonnet*, have been published in **HQ**, *Wild Weather Mouth* has been published in **A Glass of New Made Wine** (Salzburg 1999); *Chunnelend*, and *Decent Chap, Robin* were broadcast on **BBC Radio 3**; *The Bodmin Beast* and *Washing-powder War* were broadcast on **BBC Radio 4**. *The Dance of the Frogs*, translated from **The Frogs** of Aristophanes, has been published in **The Greek Theater** (Associated University Presses, 1985); *Unconquered Love*, translated from the **Antigone** of Sophocles, has been published in **Greek Poetry: New voices and Ancient Echoes** (Agenda), broadcast on **CBS** Television, and twice on **BBC** Radio 3.